wanna trade?

Carol Reinsma

Devotions for Children

wanna trade?

Carol Reinsma

Devotions for Children

CRC Publications
Grand Rapids, Michigan

Illustrations: Joy Visser

Copyright © 1995 by CRC Publications, 2850 Kalamazoo Ave. SE, Grand Rapids, Michigan 49560.

All rights reserved. With the exception of brief excerpts for review purposes, no part of this book may be reproduced in any manner whatsoever without written permission from the publisher. Printed in the United States of America on recycled paper.⊕

ISBN 1-56212-11-1

Library of Congress Cataloging-in-Publication Data
Reinsma, Carol, 1949-
    Wanna' trade? : devotions for children / Carol Reinsma.
      p.   cm.
    Summary: A book of devotions including stories from both the Bible and contemporary life.
    ISBN 1-56212-111-1
     1. Children—Prayer-books and devotions—English.
2. Christian life—Juvenile literature. [1. Prayer books and devotions.
2. Christian life.] I. Title
BV4571.2.R46   1995
242'.62—dc20   95-17545
                                                                       CIP
                                                                        AC

10 9 8 7 6 5 4 3 2 1

To my father, John Vander Kooi, one picture of my heavenly Father's love

Preface

From baseball cards to different flavors of gum, trades can be fun or disappointing. Have you ever traded something you wanted to get rid of for something you really wanted? Or have you made a trade only to realize you gave up something good for a piece of trash?

The stories in this book look at trades of all kinds. We don't know all the thoughts and actions of people in the Bible, but in this book we are imagining some of the things they might have said if they were thinking about trades. The other stories in this book are about boys and girls and the trades they've made.

As you read the stories, think about the trades you make too. And remember that the greatest trade ever made took place many years ago. Jesus traded his place in heaven to be born as a baby in a manger. And he traded his life for our sins to give us a place in heaven. That's amazing!

trade one:

A Sweet Taste *for* A Bitter Life

"Eve, come here," Adam called to me. I looked up and saw him kneeling beside a bush drooping with red berries. I could smell the sweetness before I reached him. He poured the berries into my outstretched hands.

After we ate, Adam and I sat beside the river, watching jewel-colored fish dart through the water. I dipped into the water and felt a sunny, yellow fish glide over my fingers, cool and slippery.

A tiger nuzzled me. I ran my fingers through the ripples of its stripes, ruffling its fur and smoothing it into place until it gleamed.

The next day the sun announced the morning by flinging a burst of colors through the sky. A few minutes later the ball of sunlight rose, showing off the beautiful trees, plants, and animals in God's garden.

I loved to walk in that garden talking to my husband, Adam, and my creator, God. Even our words were perfect. Never mean or angry.

Then one morning, a creature with coppery scales came to me. He told me to come with him. And I did. I followed him to the tree in the middle of the garden.

"Doesn't its fruit look good?" the creature said.

I parted the leafy branches on the tree and touched the skin of the fruit.

"It might look good," I said. "But God said, 'Do not eat from this tree.' See—we have all these other trees to eat from."

The creature smiled at me in a strange way. It made my skin tingle. Something was different and a little exciting.

"God doesn't want you to eat this fruit because it holds a secret," said the creature.

That made me curious. I moved a little closer to the creature.

"If you eat this fruit, you will be like God."

I plucked a piece off the tree. Not the biggest piece. Just a small one.

"Do you want to know as much as God?" the creature asked.

Suddenly I did. I didn't care that God said we'd die if we ate from the tree. God wouldn't really let me die, would he? Why did he give us so many wonderful things, but not this fruit? I just had to know.

I bit into the fruit. As the juice dribbled down my chin, I thought about Adam. Maybe he would like to know as much as God too. I would bring him some fruit.

Soon fruit juice was dribbling down Adam's chin too.

Then God called our names. Over and over he called. Usually when God called, we couldn't wait to talk to him. But this time we hid.

We had disobeyed God. Our God who walked with us in this beautiful, golden place. Our God who showed us new and amazing things every day.

And God asked us to leave the perfect garden.

So, you see, I traded all that I loved for one taste of fruit. When I remember that taste, it seems bitter to me. I made everything bitter when I chose not to listen to God.

I try to listen to God now, but things have changed. The bitterness is deep inside me. The only thing that gives me joy is that God still cares about us. Someday he will send a Savior to the world.

Something to Think About
How did the world change when Adam and Eve disobeyed God?

Something to Read About
You will find the story of Adam and Eve in Genesis 3.

Something to Pray About
Dear Lord, you wanted the people you made to obey you and be perfect. But instead we disobeyed you and sinned. Because you loved us, you made a plan to send Jesus, who traded his life for our sins. Thank you. Amen.

trade two:

The Wrong Present

for

A Perfect Package

Emily bounced a ball on the sidewalk. Any minute now, Dad would pull into the driveway with Aunt Tracie.

"One for Aunt Tracie, two for Aunt Tracie," sang Emily. "Aunt Tracie and me—that's the way it's going to be."

Dad's car pulled into the driveway, and Emily bounced with the ball.

Aunt Tracie stepped out of the car and gave Emily a big hug. "How's your mom?" asked Aunt Tracie.

"I thought you came here to worry about me," Emily said.

Aunt Tracie gave Emily a warm squeeze. "Of course I did. But I'm here to help your mom too. She'll need us when the baby is born."

Emily dug her toes into a sidewalk crack while Dad and Aunt Tracie carried in the suitcases. She waited, wondering when they'd notice she was still outside. When no one came, Emily tiptoed up to the front door. She listened. It was very quiet inside the house. Without making a noise, she slipped inside.

Voices were coming from the new nursery. Emily plopped herself down on the sofa. She blew air on her face, making her bangs flip off her forehead. Everyone said she looked like Aunt Tracie. But maybe something had changed, and it wasn't true anymore.

She got up to check in the mirror. On her way to the bathroom, she saw the suitcases in the hallway. Two suitcases, and one of them had bulging sides. Did Aunt Tracie bring her a present?

Zlup, zlup—Emily slid the zipper open. Her fingers touched the glossy sides of a box wrapped in pink and blue paper.

She wriggled the fat box out of the zippered opening. She shook the box close to her ear. Thump and thud. More than two things were inside. She was sure.

Then she heard a different kind of noise. Someone was coming! There wasn't time to squeeze the box back into the suitcase. Quickly she opened the closet door and shoved the box inside.

"There you are, Emily," said Aunt Tracie. "Let's take my suitcase to the guest room. Then you and I can make our special plans."

Emily reached for the suitcase with the open zipper.

"No, you take this little one," said Aunt Tracie.

Emily kept her eyes on the open zipper all the way to the guest room.

"I'm going to play now," Emily said after they had put the suitcases down.

She ran downstairs and hid in the closet with the present. She blew out a long breath of air. Then she pressed her ear against the door, listening.

Soft-soled shoes scooted past the crack at the bottom of the closet door. Aunt Tracie. Now was the time to sneak the present back into the suitcase.

She opened the door a crack. Voices.

"You should call the airline," Mom was saying. "It's not right that someone opened your bag and stole the present."

Emily closed the door and sat on the closet floor. It was too late to return the present. She held the box close to her heart. It'd be a shame not to enjoy her present.

Her fingertips peeled the paper away from the taped edges. Then she lifted off the lid. Containers of baby shampoo, powder, and lotion rested on a soft pink and blue blanket. A baby gift! Aunt Tracie wasn't even thinking about her.

Emily stuffed the baby gift behind the winter boots.

She left the closet, switched on the TV, and pretended to watch it.

Aunt Tracie came into the TV room holding something behind her back. "I have a present for my Emily." She held out a box with purple wrapping paper.

"For me?" asked Emily. "Not for the baby?"

"The baby's present was stolen," said Aunt Tracie.

Emily hid her face behind her hands.

"What's wrong?" asked Aunt Tracie.

"Purple packages are for girls who are better than me," said Emily.

After a trip to the closet, Aunt Tracie said, "I wish you had trusted me to give you what I had planned."

"Please forgive me," Emily said.

"I have an idea," Aunt Tracie said. "After the baby is born, let's make a trade. When you're ready to give the baby its gift, I'll give you the purple package."

Emily took the baby things to her room and drew pictures on the gift box to make it look pretty. She put the package on her dresser, and every day she waited for the baby to be born.

Something to Think About
How did Emily feel when Aunt Tracie brought her the purple package?

Something to Read About
Read Matthew 7: 9-12.

Something to Pray About
Dear Lord, help us not to think only about ourselves. Show us how to love others as you love us. Help us to trust you for all things. Amen.

trade three:

Years of Right *for* Months of Animals

It was a hot day. I took a break from pulling weeds and rested under the shade of an olive tree.

"Noah," whispered a voice.

I knew it was God. I was glad he came to talk to me.

"I'm going to send rain," God said.

"Thanks, we can use a good shower. It's been hot and dry."

"No, I mean rain that doesn't stop. It will rain for forty days and forty nights."

"Whoa," I said. "That much rain sounds like a washout."

"Yes," God said. "It'll destroy everything."

I gulped. "But what about my home? My family?"

"I have a plan," God said. "I want you to build an ark. I'll give you all the instructions you need. This ark will hold your family and two of every kind of animal. So when I send the rain, everyone inside the ark will be safe. You'll live in the ark until the water dries up on the earth."

"It'd take me years to build something like that. I don't know. . ."

"Noah, do you believe my words are true?"

"Yes, Lord."

"Then what are you going to do?"

I searched the sky for one cloud. Not even a wisp of a cloud floated in the blue above.

"When you send the rain, couldn't you pluck up my family and set us on a mountain?"

"No, I want you to do it my way, Noah. I'm saving you and your family, but no one else. No one else on earth listens to me and believes my words are true."

I thought about my neighbors. God was right about that.

"Tell me what to do, and I'll get started," I said.

Once I heard the instructions, I knew that life as I had known it was over. What a trade—all these years of obeying God, and he makes a deal with me to build a ridiculous ark in the middle of the land. You'd think he'd offer some kind of reward that would make my neighbors see I chose the right way to live.

My sons and I began gathering supplies. We needed so many things that my land looked like a lumberyard. People came from miles around to see what I was doing. As the thing began to take shape, many people recognized it as an ark. Then the laughter and mocking started. My ark was the joke of the year.

"This is what you get for praying to your God," they said.

I didn't say much. After all, the silliest part was still to come.

And it did. After months of building, my sons and I went in search of the animals to fill the ark. As we gathered them up, two by two, I again thought, what a trade! Years serving the Lord, and he saves my life like this! It's true that God made the animals obey me—it wasn't hard at all to get them on the ark. But why couldn't he do something spectacular? Why did he choose a way that made everyone laugh at me?

Finally I closed the big doors of the ark. Then the rain started, and it didn't stop for forty days. The water got so deep that it even covered the mountains. But my family and I stayed safe and dry. The ark didn't let in one drop. I had the safest feeling on that ark—almost like God was rocking us in his hands.

After the rain finally stopped, we still had a long wait. It took months before the water dried up from the earth. Then one day, the ark struck the mountain, and there we sat. I sent out a raven to see if it could find a resting place. Later I sent out a dove. And when it brought back an olive leaf, I knew my family and I would be able to leave the ark soon.

Finally our day came, and I stood in wonder at the sight of the newly green earth. Maybe it was months of being cooped up with animals, but I had never smelled anything so sweet.

Then God put a rainbow in the sky and told us it was a sign of his promise never to flood the earth again. The rainbow stretched from one end of the earth to the other. The arch of colors glowed above us. And then I knew my part of the trade was small. God *had* done something amazing!

Something to Think About

What do you think is most wonderful about the way God saved Noah?

Something to Read About

You can read about Noah in Genesis 6-9.

Something to Pray About

Lord, you made a promise to Noah, and you kept it. You also promised to send your Son to save us. You kept that promise too. Each day help us to remember your promises to love us and to come again. Amen.

trade four:

A Little Squirt *for* A Big Splash

It was firecracker hot the day after the fourth of July. There were no more picnics or parades to look forward to, but I promised my little sister, Sarah, we would have fun anyway. I filled three wading pools with water. I unrolled a long, plastic sheet and aimed the hose so the water ran down the plastic slide. Next, I filled twenty balloons with water and loaded two squirt guns.

As I adjusted the sprinkler, my friend, Anna, climbed over the fence from her yard into mine.

"Hey, Lisa, what are you doing?" Anna called to me.

"Making a water park," I yelled.

"Not much of a water park," Anna said. "You'd get wetter and cooler at the public swimming pool."

I shrugged. "I'm making this water park for my little sister, Sarah."

Anna picked up a squirt gun. She squeezed the trigger. "I'll trade my swimming pool pass for this squirt gun."

Water from the hose trickled over my feet. I could picture myself sliding down the twisting slide with aqua-blue water shooting me into the pool with a big splash.

Anna twirled the squirt gun waiting for an answer. "Michelle, Cori, and Rachelle will be at the pool."

I turned off the hose nozzle. "Maybe Sarah could wait until tomorrow."

Anna grinned. She tucked the barrel of the squirt gun into her belt.

Just then Sarah skipped out of the back door in her orange swimsuit.

"No, wait. I can't trade," I said. "Sarah and I need two squirt guns to play our game."

Anna stared at me and Sarah for a minute, then threw the squirt gun on the grass. "Your loss," she said, walking out of my yard.

Sarah ran from one pool to the next and giggled all the way down the slippery slide. She was getting wet and cool.

But I was hot and only wet below my knees. Maybe it wasn't too late. I could tell Anna I changed my mind.

"Sarah," I called. "Are you having fun?"

She shook the water out of her hair like a puppy. "The best," she said.

"Good, slip on the slide again. I'm going somewhere. I'll be back."

"When are we going to have our water gun fight?" she asked.

"How about tomorrow?" I said. "We don't want to do all the fun things in one day."

The back gate squeaked behind me. I stood in the alley waiting and listening. Sarah had quit laughing and running through the water.

Slowly I walked toward Anna's house, still listening for Sarah. But the afternoon was as quiet as it is when all the kids are reading in school.

For some reason Anna and the public pool didn't sound as exciting as it had in my backyard. I stood a minute outside Anna's gate, then turned around and ran home.

When I got there, Sarah's back was toward me. Sliding through the grass, I crept up behind her and squirted her with a big blast.

"You tricked me," she laughed. "I should have guessed you were up to a surprise. You're the best sister."

She pulled her trigger and chased me around the yard right into the nest of water balloons. Most of them popped, soaking me from head to toe. I looked up through the spray of the sprinkler and saw the colors of the rainbow.

I was glad I'd kept my promise to Sarah.

Something to Think About
How do you think Lisa felt after she left Sarah alone and headed toward Lisa's house?

Something to Read About
And to your service for God, add kindness for your brothers and sisters in Christ; and to this kindness add love. *2 Peter 1:7*

Something to Pray About
Dear Lord, thank you for always keeping your promises to us. Thank you for loving us too. Help us show love to others. Amen.

trade five:

A Blessing *for* Soup

"Esau, quit wrestling with your brother." My mother said that to me so many times that I almost quit listening.

It was fun wrestling with Jacob because I was stronger than him. With a few fast moves, I could pin him down. The only time he'd get *me* down is when he'd sneak up behind me, grab me by the ankle, and trip me. Mom said he had been doing that to me since the day we were born.

When I wasn't wrestling, I liked to hunt. Leaving the green grass and the wells that surrounded our tent, I climbed up the rocky hillside. The goats up there were not like the ones grazing on our grass. These goats scrambled around looking for juicy bits of green blades between the rocks. They also took off at the sight of me. I learned to leap over the rocks as quickly as they could, outsmarting them at their own games. The deer couldn't escape my swift feet and fast arrows either.

Dad beamed with pride when I carried home deer meat. As the meat sizzled over the fire, the air filled with mouth-watering scents. "Son, there is nothing I like better than your smoked deer meat," said my father, putting his arm around my shoulder.

One day I went hunting as usual, but didn't have much luck. By noontime, I still didn't have a deer. The sun beat down on my back, and hunger pains chewed away in my stomach. So I made my way down the hillside to my family's tent, thinking I would hunt again in the evening.

There, under the cool shade of a tree was my brother, Jacob, stirring something in a pot over the fire. Boy, it smelled good!

"Give me some of that soup," I said.

Jacob looked at me with one of those funny grins that he often wore when he'd sneak up on me. "I'll sell it to you for your birthright."

As the oldest son, I had the first right to all of Dad's belongings. But that didn't seem very important right now. Who needs a few tame goats and cattle anyway? There are plenty of wild ones up in the hills. And I could always live in a cave.

So Jacob and I made the deal. I filled my stomach with the soup and bread. Now I was full of energy again and ready to hunt down my deer.

One day, my father called to me. "Esau, prepare me a meal of deer meat. Bring it to me so I can bless you before I die."

I hurried up the hillside. This was going to be my day. I'd get blessings and riches from my father. Jacob probably didn't even remember that I sold the birthright to him.

I was so eager to return to my father that I didn't look for the biggest buck. Quickly, I chose a slow-moving, old one. I cooked up the meat and hurried into Father's tent.

"Who are you?" my blind father asked.

"I am your son, your firstborn, Esau."

Father trembled at my words. "Who was it, then, that brought food to me earlier. I already blessed him."

Suddenly, I realized what had happened. That sneaky, trickster of a brother. I yelled at my father. "Bless me—me too!"

But he couldn't. It was out of his hands. The blessing was from God. All my father could do was pass it along. And he had already done that—to Jacob.

I had traded God's blessing for a bowl of soup. But it was all Jacob's fault—he tricked me.

Well, we'll just see if God *really* blesses Jacob.

Something to Think About
How did Esau lose God's blessing?

Something to Read About
You can read the first part of Esau and Jacob's story in Genesis 25:21-34.

Something to Pray About
Lord, help me to put you and your blessings before anything else in my life. Amen.

trade six:

Lots of Toys

for

A Couple Hours of Fun

Every year, men with wide suspenders and greasy hats set up a carnival in the shopping center parking lot. Last year, George went with his twin brother, Alex. But it was a short day. With their allowance, they had only enough for three rides—and George wanted to ride all day long.

"This year it will be different," George said to Alex. "I'm going to have enough money to ride until the gates close."

"Have you saved any money?" asked Alex.

George didn't answer. Instead he pulled out his in-line skates and football from under his bed. "I'll sell everything," he said. "Then I'll have enough money."

He spread out his belongings on the front yard. Then he made signs that read: *Big Sports and Game Sale 1065 2nd Street.* He put the signs on five street corners.

Fifteen minutes later, boys and girls of all ages came to George's big sale.

In an hour George's dinosaur collection was gone. So were his baseball cards, ball, bat, and glove. All that was left was a tiny, orange car with a missing wheel.

George skipped to the carnival with the money heavy inside his pockets. Alex followed George. After Alex finished his first three rides with George, he waited for George after each ride. Sometimes George took the same ride three or four times in a row.

"Did you see me, Alex?" George asked when he came off the roller coaster. "I was the one with my arms straight up in the air at the very top."

George ran to the bumper cars. "Watch me," he yelled to Alex.

He hit every car in his path. "Kaboom, kaboom. Did you see me, Alex?"

When George had only fifty cents left, he bought a lemonade. He drank it in one long gulp. "Rides make you very thirsty," he said to Alex, who was feeling thirsty too.

When they got home, Alex called Jason on the phone.

Jason and Alex traded baseball cards.

George watched.

After an hour, Jason went home.

"Do you want to trade baseball cards with me?" asked George.

"You don't have any cards to trade." Alex said, leaving the room.

George watched as Alex put on his skates and went outside. "Can I come too?" he asked.

"You don't have skates anymore," said Alex.

George sat on the lawn and watched Alex and the other kids play street hockey.

By evening George was feeling kind of sick. He hadn't realized how much fun he was trading for his good time at the carnival.

When Alex took a puzzle out after supper, George looked away.

"Do you want to make this puzzle with me?" Alex asked.

George blew his breath through his lips. "I sold all my puzzles," he said, his lip trembling a little.

"Well, it's a good thing you didn't sell me," Alex said with a grin. "You may not have many toys left, but at least you have me to play with." He dumped the puzzle pieces on the kitchen table.

As George sat down and started looking for pieces of the sky, the sick feeling in his stomach began to go away.

Something to Think About
How did George feel after the carnival?

Something to Read About
You can read more about Jacob and Esau in Genesis 27:1-40.

Something to Pray About
Dear Lord, thank you for giving us people who love us and will forgive us when we make bad choices. Help us to show love to others. Amen.

trade seven:

work

for

Love

I enjoyed living at home, but after I tricked my brother, Esau, out of my father's blessing, I had to run. Mother arranged for me to spend some time with my Uncle Laban in the east. I had never even visited my mother's family for a holiday, and now here I was on my way to live with them.

When I came near Haran, I asked some shepherds if they knew my Uncle Laban.

"Here comes his daughter Rachel," they said.

I looked where they were pointing. And then I smiled. She was beautiful!

I watched Rachel for a minute as she dropped her buckets near the well, and then I hurried over to her. Like all deep wells, this one had a rock covering the opening so animals couldn't fall into it. I rolled the rock away for Rachel, filled her buckets, and gave water to her sheep. She smiled at my enthusiasm for her job. Actually it wasn't the job I was eager for; I wanted Rachel to like me.

And she did! Rachel ran home to tell her father about me.

Before long, Uncle Laban sent for me. He greeted me with a hug. "So you're Rebecca's son, Jacob," he said. "We'd be honored to have you stay with us. Our family is your family."

"I left home with nothing," I said.

"Don't worry, son," Uncle Laban said. "My flocks and herds are growing in number. Work for me, and I'll pay you with anything of mine that you desire."

I didn't have to think about that one. I knew what trade would be worth working for from sunup until sundown—the opportunity to marry Rachel!

We agreed on the terms. For seven years, I'd work for Uncle Laban. Then I'd marry Rachel.

Every day of those seven years, I talked to Rachel. I lived for the smile to light up her face. Sometimes I'd even watch her when she didn't know it. The way she talked and moved made me love her even more.

Her older sister, Leah, sometimes tried to take my attention away from Rachel. Leah would fix my favorite dinner or set out cool water for my aching shepherd feet. I appreciated Leah, but it was the smile and touch of Rachel that I dreamed about.

After seven years of work, I was ready to collect on my trade. The wedding date was notched on my shepherd's staff. During the ceremony, I couldn't see Rachel under the veil of her wedding garments, but I could picture her smile in my mind. In a few minutes she would become Mrs. Jacob!

When the ceremony was over, I turned to lift her veil and look into her beautiful eyes. But the eyes that looked back at me were not Rachel's. They were Leah's!

"Uncle Laban," I cried. "You've tricked me. What happened to our trade?!"

"It is not our way to marry the younger daughter before the older one," he said. "If you work for me for seven more years, you can marry Rachel too."

What could I do? I couldn't take back the marriage vows made under oath. It was like the passing of God's blessing to me from my father. As soon as Isaac blessed me instead of Esau, it was over. No matter how much Esau begged father, the blessing belonged to me.

Now I knew that being tricked felt miserable. Is that how Esau felt too? I wished that I had trusted God back then instead of tricking my brother.

I knew that the next seven years wouldn't be easy. But I asked God to teach me patience.

Something to Think About
Jacob ran away with God's blessing. But things aren't going so well. Is God really going to bless Jacob?

Something to Read About
You can read about Jacob in Genesis 29.

Something to Pray About
Dear Lord, help me to trust you no matter what happens—good or bad. Thank you for always taking care of me. Amen.

trade eight:

Work *for* A Good Time

Jack and his cousins Willy and Drake sat on the grass by the stream. Grandpa was at the cabin fixing lunch.

The boys took off their socks and shoes and inched their way into the cold mountain stream.

"There goes a rainbow trout," Jack said.

"We could catch the trout if we had poles and bait," Willy said.

"But who's going to get the poles?" Drake asked.

"I will," Jack said.

He ran to the cabin and came back with three poles and a jar of bait.

"I'm not going to put the bait on the hook," said Drake.

"Neither am I," said Willy.

So Jack put the bait on the hooks and handed the poles to Willy and Drake.

The hungry fish snapped at the bait. One little fish snapped too hard. He was caught on Willy's hook. Drake caught the second little one. The small fish flopped on the dock while Jack trailed his line through the stream. Finally a big fish bit hard, and Jack snagged it. He took his fish off the hook, put his line back in the water, and waited for more.

A few minutes passed, and then Jack caught an even bigger fish. It flipped and flopped as Jack struggled to get the hook out of its mouth.

"This one's for Grandpa," Jack said.

Willy and Drake stood beside their little fish.

"Aren't you going to take the fish off your hooks?" Jack asked.

"No way," said Willy.

"Me neither," said Drake.

So Jack took the little fish off the hooks. "Who's going to clean the fish?" Jack asked.

"Not me," said Willy.

"Not me," said Drake.

So Jack cleaned the fish and carried them back to the cabin with the fishing poles.

"You caught some beauties," said Grandpa when he saw the fish.

Willy and Drake were still down by the stream.

So Jack stacked the firewood.

Grandpa found a pan for the fish. He struck a match on a stone and held the match on the wood until it caught on fire.

When the fire was just right, Grandpa and Jack put the pan of fish on the grill.

Willy and Drake came running at the smell of pan-fried fish.

"Salad, rolls, and iced tea are in the cabin," said Grandpa. "Who will get the rest of our lunch?"

Willy and Drake sat on the picnic bench.

"We're tired," said Willy.

So Jack went to get the food. When he came out, Drake was boasting to Grandpa. "Catching big fish is easy for me," Drake said.

"What's your secret?" asked Grandpa.

"Talking to the fish in a loud voice," Drake said.

"Hmm," said Grandpa. "Jack, do you have a secret way to catch big fish?"

"I wait quietly," Jack said.

Grandpa winked at Jack.

Willy and Drake took big helpings of everything.

"So," said Grandpa. "Next weekend I want to hike up the mountain. We'll sleep in the tent. Who wants to go with me?"

"I do," shouted Drake.

"I do," shouted Willy.

"I do," said Jack.

"Hmm," said Grandpa. "The tent is only big enough for one person besides me. Now who will I choose?" He took off his glasses and wiped them on his flannel shirt. Then he looked at each one of the boys.

"I know," he said. "I'll take the boy who works the hardest. I'll take Jack."

And he did.

Something to Think About
Why did Grandpa choose Jack to go on the hiking trip with him?

Something to Read About
In all the work you are doing, work the best you can. Work as if you were doing it for the Lord, not for people. *Colossians 3:23*

Something to Pray About
Dear Lord, help us to honor you in our work and play. Amen.

trade nine:

A Brother *for* Silver

"Joseph," my father called to me. "Your brothers have been gone many days. I'm worried about them. Put on your sandals, and go search for them."

It wasn't so strange for my brothers to be gone. Our family had huge flocks of sheep, so we often had to go in search of new pastures to feed them all. My father, Jacob, said God had blessed us and that one day we would be a great nation.

I wondered if the strange dreams I had been having had something to do with God's promises. I dreamed that my brothers all bowed down to me—Joseph! Did it mean I would be a king someday?

You can imagine how my brothers reacted when I told them about that dream. Almost the same way they reacted when father gave me a beautiful new coat.

Everyone said Father loves me best, and I guess it might be true. You see, my brothers are all Leah's children. But I was born to Rachel, and Rachel is my father's favorite wife.

But back to my story. The day my father sent me to find my brothers, I was wearing the beautiful coat that had made my brothers so jealous. And I was feeling pretty good about myself. When I passed a stream, I stopped to admire my reflection in the water. Then I traveled on.

As I came close to the grazing place where I thought I might find my brothers, I heard a hoarse whisper from behind a bush. "There he is. Grab him."

My brothers had seen me coming from a distance and decided to get even with me. And I didn't have a chance against them. They were older, and there were more of them. Their loud voices rang in my ear.

"Strip the coat off of him."

"Don't let him kick you."

"On the count of three, toss him into the opening."

"We'll never have to hear him or his dreams again."

Suddenly, I was falling down a dark hole. I landed hard in a foot of oozing mud. An old well! The round circle of light far above me disappeared. Tiny pieces of sand showered down on me. My brothers had covered the well opening with a rock. How was God going to get me out of this? Did he really have a plan for me?

Above the faint laughter of my brother's voices, I felt a heavy pounding of something against the earth. It stopped. More loud voices, then some yelling. Someone slid the cover off my prison and dropped down a rope. A rescue plan already? That was fast. I scrambled up the rope, but it wasn't to freedom that I climbed. In a matter of seconds, I was put in chains and tied to the back of a supply-carrying camel.

"Lord, this plan doesn't seem like a smart idea," I mumbled. "These men will take me to a far-off place. What about the dream you sent me? How will it ever come true now?"

One of the traders opened a money pouch. He poured twenty silver coins into the hands of my eager brothers. My brothers, who shared all the wealth of my father, traded me for a measly twenty pieces of silver.

All my dreams were fading. I thought God had great plans for my future. Could I still trust him?

In my mind, I dug deep into all the things my father told me about God. "God always keeps his promises," Father said, "even when it seems impossible."

I knew I had to remember that—no matter what.

Something to Think About

Was it easy for Joseph to trust God when he lived with his Father? After he had been sold to the traders? When is it hard for you to trust God?

Something to Read About

You can read this story about Joseph in Genesis 37.

Something to Pray About

Dear Lord, sometimes when we're hurt or afraid, it's hard to trust you. Help us remember that you always keep your promises. Amen.

trade ten:

Trouble
for
Good

"During which of the four seasons is the sun nearest the earth?" asked Mrs. Smiley, the third grade teacher.

David raised his hand first.

"Yes, David, what's the answer?"

"Summer," said David. "I can tell because that's when it's the hottest."

"Who thinks David is right?"

All the hands went up except Reginald's.

"What is the answer, Reginald?" asked Mrs. Smiley.

Reginald stood beside his desk. "The sun is nearest to the earth during the winter. The reason we don't get as much heat is because the rays come down slantwise on the northern hemisphere, distributing their heat over much more surface."

"Excellent!" said Mrs. Smiley. "I can always depend on you for the right answer."

"The answer was in our science books," Reginald whispered to David. "I read our assignment."

"Well, goody good for you," David said.

At recess time, a group of boys gathered around David.

Reginald tossed his football, catching it before it touched the ground. "Are you fellows in the mood for a rousing game of 500?" he asked.

No one answered. They huddled closer together, ignoring Reginald.

Reginald tossed his football higher, playing a game with himself. Soon he was throwing the ball too far to reach it before it touched the ground.

"What's the matter?" called David. "Can't the teacher's pet catch his own ball?"

"I'm not the teacher's pet," Reginald said. "I just try to learn the most I can from every subject."

"I'll bet he calls the teacher every night and gets the questions ahead of time," Jeffy smirked.

"That's ridiculous," Reginald said.

"Did he call us stupid?" asked David.

"I think so," Jeffy said. "Let's get him."

On the count of three, the group of boys tackled Reginald. They knocked him to the ground. Reginald wrestled and kicked to get free. The other boys kicked back. Soon no one knew who was kicking whom. Fists and feet were flying in all directions.

Wheeet, wheet, went the playground teacher's whistle. "Stop now," she called. "All of you boys get up and march to the principal's office."

With torn shirts, streaks of dirt, and bowed heads, the boys stood in front of the principal.

"Who started this?" Mr. Grimm, the principal, asked.

All heads were bowed. No one answered.

"I need an answer," Mr. Grimm demanded.

David lifted his head. "Reginald started calling us names. We didn't want to fight but . . ."

"What did he call you?"

"Things like stupid. I don't remember it all, but he was making us mad."

"I see," said Mr. Grimm.

"Everyone except for Reginald go back to class."

The boys filed out one by one, their heads humbly bowed until they were safely down the hallway.

"Yes," David cheered in a loud whisper. "We got him."

The other boys slapped David's raised hand.

Back in the principal's office, Reginald held his throbbing arm.

"What do you have to say for yourself?" asked Mr. Grimm.

"It is simply a clear case of misunderstanding," Reginald said. "They exchanged my very words for what they wanted to hear."

"They wanted to hear you call them bad names?" asked Mr. Grimm. "That sounds strange."

"No," said Reginald. "*I* said ridiculous. They *thought* I said stupid."

"Ridiculous or stupid—it makes no difference. I will not allow name calling. Report to my office after school today." Mr. Grimm scribbled a note to Mrs. Smiley. "Give this to your teacher so she knows what is happening."

On the way back to class, Reginald wanted to tear up the note. Then he decided he'd tell Mrs. Smiley the real story instead. David and his friends would be in double trouble when the truth came out.

That will serve them right, thought Reginald, slapping his hand on Mrs. Smiley's door. Then he frowned. *But it sure won't make them like me.*

TO BE CONTINUED

Something to Think About
Who really started the fight? Why?

Something to Read About
I say to you who are listening to me, love your enemies, do good to those who hate you. *Luke 6:27*

Something to Pray About
Lord, help us to care about people who hate us. And thank you for always loving us—even when we don't deserve it. Amen.

trade eleven:

Strangers *for* Brothers

They came on dusty, mangy camels. They came on blistered feet. They came bringing me their gold, silver, and pearls for a cup of flour.

I was their hope for life, for survival. I controlled the only source of food in all of Egypt and the surrounding countries. The cracks in the dried up earth grew wider as the lines outside my palace doors grew longer.

This morning was like any other.

"Oh, please great Zaphnath-Paaneah, fill my sack with grain. I don't have anything to give you except my worthless land. Take it so my children can live."

"How many in your family?" I asked.

"Just my wife and two children."

"Keep your land. My servant will fill your sack."

The next man hid behind a veil.

"Haven't you been here every day this week?" I asked.

"No, my most honored Governor. You are wise, handsome, and all-powerful, but you've never seen me before."

"Guards, look at this man. Is he the one you followed home yesterday and the day before?"

"He's the one," said a guard.

"Then throw him in prison," I ordered. How angry the cheaters made me!

I looked at the crowd of people still waiting. Who else would come today? A group of sun-weathered shepherds from a far country stood a few feet down the line. Not too unusual, but shepherds always caught my attention.

The curly, redheaded one and the tall dark-haired one made me stop and look again. Could it be? My heart pounded. They were older and thinner, but these ten men had to be my brothers.

Suddenly I wished I could shed my Egyptian garments and name and become Joseph again. I wanted to run and hug my brothers.

Then the pictures of dark wells, a camel trip to Egypt, and prison flashed through my mind. It was these men standing in my palace who had taken my father from me.

Were my brothers any different than all the other dishonest men who stood before me? Once they had been willing to kill and lie because of their hate for me. Were they any different today?

I was sure they wouldn't recognize me—not dressed like an Egyptian ruler. They'd never guess that I was the one who told Pharaoh the meaning of his troubling dreams. Or that it was my plan to save food from the times of plenty for these times of famine.

My brother Simeon spoke. "We have come for food."

"More likely you are spies," I said.

"We're not spies," Simeon said fearfully. "We are brothers. There are twelve of us. One is gone and the other is home with Father."

The truth from their lips shocked me. I was so shaken that I ordered them thrown into prison. I had to have time to think and come up with plans to test them.

Three days later, I sent nine of them home. "If you are who you say you are, you will return with your youngest brother."

The day they returned with Benjamin brought tears to my eyes. Benjamin hadn't even been old enough to shave when I left home. Now he was a tall, grown man. He had eyes like my mother's. Were my older brothers jealous and mean to him like they had been to me?

I wanted to find out so I hid my silver cup in Benjamin's sack. Then, as my brothers were leaving town, I sent my servant after them. The servant dug my cup out of Benjamin's sack.

"This thief will be my master's slave," said my servant.

My brothers came begging to me. "Make us slaves instead," they pleaded. "It will kill our father if something happens to Benjamin."

Then I knew they *had* changed! They were willing to take the punishment for Benjamin.

I stripped off my Egyptian head covering. "I am your brother, Joseph," I told them with tears in my eyes.

They trembled as if waiting to be killed.

But I hugged them. "You meant to hurt me," I said. "But God took your evil plans and brought me to this place so I could save you from starving to death."

Something to Think About

Was God with Joseph in Egypt? How do you know?

Something to Read About

You can read about Joseph in Genesis 42-45.

Something to Pray About

Lord, thank you for caring for us always—even when everything seems to be going wrong. You take bad things and turn them into good things. Help us always to trust you. Amen.

trade twelve:

From Reginald

to

Reggie

The classroom became instantly quiet when Reginald walked through the door. Stiffly he stepped up to Mrs. Smiley's desk.

He held out the note from Mr. Grimm. "The official statement from the office of disciplinary action," he said quietly.

"I see," said Mrs. Smiley. "The other boys told me you were making fun of them because they didn't know the answers in class."

Reginald sneaked a quick look at David. He seemed to be taming a wild smile from jumping across his face.

Mrs. Smiley continued, "I'll give you a chance to speak if you have another side to the story."

Reginald lifted his head far enough to see if David still looked pleased with himself. No, his smile was gone now. His face was as flat as Roadrunner after Coyote runs over him.

"I-I don't know." Reginald stumbled over his words. "It happened so fast."

Mrs. Smiley opened the note. "Mr. Grimm says you were involved in name-calling. I am disappointed in you, Reginald. You've never acted like this before. I don't understand what made you do it."

Reginald didn't say anything. With his head down he walked to his seat. He wanted to close his eyes to hold back the tears, but his right eye throbbed.

Someone coughed. Then it was silent again. Silent as during test time.

Most of the kids got busy and worked on their math problems. But Reginald couldn't concentrate. He caught David looking at him several times. And he thought he noticed something different in David's face. His eyes didn't seem to mock Reginald like they had before.

When the second recess bell rang, David stopped by Reginald's desk. "How's your eye?" David asked.

Reginald touched his right eye. It felt swollen and tender.

"I could get you ice from the nurse's office," David said.

Reginald nodded. "Ice should reduce some swelling. Thank you."

David ran off. He returned panting and carrying the ice. "Guess you're going to get a black eye," David said. "I had one before. It's kind of neat. Everyone makes a fuss over you."

Reginald smiled. He waited for David to run off and join the other kids. But he didn't.

"Why didn't you tell Mrs. Smiley it was my fault?" David finally asked. "She would have believed you. After all, she likes you the best."

"I'm not sure," Reginald said quietly. "I planned to, but somehow the words didn't come out. I guess I couldn't see any sense in getting all of you in trouble. It's not much fun, you know—I found out! Besides—," he looked down shyly, "I was hoping we could be friends."

David looked embarassed. "Yeah—I guess we've been kind of hard on you. It's because you're so smart. You always know the answers. Maybe you didn't call us stupid, but you make us *feel* stupid."

"I'm no smarter than you are, David," Reginald said.

"Aw—come on. You're just saying that," David said.

"It's true," said Reginald. "I just know Mrs. Smiley's tricks."

"What do you mean?" wondered David.

"When Mrs. Smiley asks a question, you have to be careful. The answer isn't what you might think at first," Reginald explained.

"How do you know?" asked David.

"Think about this question," Reginald said. "Would a marble fall faster through water at 70 degrees Fahrenhite or at 10 degrees Fahrenhite?"

"Water is water," David said.

"Think."

"Oh yeah," David said. "Water freezes at 32 degrees Fahrenhite. I get what you're saying. Think before I answer. Do you think Mrs. Smiley will really like me if I start giving her the right answers?"

"It has been my passage to her heart," Reginald said, smiling.

"I could never talk like you, though."

Reginald sighed. "If I talked more like you, would the fellows play football with me?"

"Guys!" David said. "Call them guys, and they'll play with you. I'll make sure of it. We could even call you Reggie."

"Reggie it is," Reginald said, following David onto the playground.

Something to Think About
How did David feel when Reginald didn't tell Mrs. Smiley what really happened on the playground?

Something to Read About
Do you have mercy and kindness? If so, make me very happy by having the same thoughts, sharing the same love, and having one mind and purpose.
Philippians 2:1b-2

Something to Pray About
Dear Lord, we make you happy when we care about others. Through your Holy Spirit, fill us with love and kindness. Amen.

trade thirteen:

Dazzling Stones *for* Sand

Most people would have traded places with me. After all, I lived in a palace. As the son of the princess, whatever I wanted was mine. The palace walls sparkled with gold coverings. Red and turquoise stones decorated pillars and floors, and I wore bright jewels around my neck. Cool and fragrant gardens bloomed on the palace grounds. Who could want anything more?

But the wealth of palaces and gardens didn't mean much when my heart ached for something else. I wanted freedom for the slaves. I knew that without the slaves, my life of luxury in the palace wouldn't be possible. So, the sensible thing would have been to turn my back on their pains. Why let their troubles bother me? But from the shape of their noses and the color of their skin, I knew they were my true family. I wanted to belong to them and their God instead of to the Egyptians and their pretend gods.

I remembered another mother from long ago, when I was just beginning to walk and talk. That mother disobeyed the orders of Pharaoh, the ruler of Egypt. Pharaoh ordered all baby boys to be drowned in the Nile River. But my mother put me in a basket instead of drowning me. And when the princess found me while she was bathing in the river, she kept me and made me her own son. She named me Moses which means "drawn out of the water."

For the first few years, the princess hired my real mom to care for me. During this time, my mother wrapped her arms around me and told me stories. She told me about God and a man named Joseph.

Many Pharaohs later it was hard to find anyone who remembered Joseph. The Egyptians forgot that it was Joseph who saved them from starving by storing up food before the years of no rain and no crops. But God didn't forget about Joseph and his brothers. He blessed their families, and they grew into a great nation—the Israelites.

This great nation frightened the Pharaoh of Egypt. So he made the Israelites his slaves. My people had been slaves for many years—first for that Pharaoh and then for the Pharaohs who followed him.

The Pharaoh who ruled now was my adopted grandfather. At night, he dreamed of ways to make life harder for his slaves. Down the hall from Pharaoh, I dreamed of ways to trade in my linen clothes and jewels to help my people.

The cutting slashes of a whip snapped outside my window. A slave master was whipping an Israelite!

"Put down the whip," I yelled. "You've no right to beat a person. Slave or not."

"Mind your own business, Moses," said the slave master. "Why are you such a slave lover anyway?"

Anger rose hot inside of me. I couldn't watch one of God's people, my people, being hurt worse than usual.

So I jumped the slave master. And in the struggle, I killed him. Quickly, I buried him, then looked around. Did anyone see me?

The next day, the palace buzzed with the news of the dead slave master. I heard my name whispered in the banquet room. Pharaoh called his soldiers into the throne room. The sharpening of swords told me it was time to run. And fast.

Without packing or even filling up a goat-skin water bag, I left the shaded streets of the city. I ran to the most hopeless place I could think of—the desert. I didn't mind trading the dazzling stones and jewels of a prince for a life of walking through the hot sand in the desert. But I knew that hiding in the desert wasn't helping my people.

"Dear God, don't forget the Israelites," I prayed every day.

God led me to a family of shepherds. I made my home with them, worked for them, and told them the ways of my God.

Every day, as I searched the desert for water and grass for my sheep, I thanked God for giving me food and drink. If only he would provide a way out of Egypt for his people.

Something to Think About
Was it easier for Moses to trust God when he lived in Egypt or when he lived in the desert? Why?

Something to Read About
The story of Moses can be found in Exodus 2.

Something to Pray About
Dear Lord, we know you were with Moses—even in the desert. Thank you for being with us too—even when we're sick or lonely or afraid. Help us to trust you always. Amen.

trade fourteen:

A Lightweight Car

for

A Light Heart

Max ran his finger over the glossy red surface of his pinewood derby car.

"This is the greatest car. It could be a first-place winner."

Dad grinned. "We worked hard. I hope Benny's car turned out sharp too. His mother told me last Sunday that he put his whole heart into his car."

"Dad! His car'll never compete with mine. He doesn't have the tools we have. How could he sand his wheels smooth without a drill to spin them?"

"It's possible to sand them by hand," Dad said as he pulled into the church parking lot.

Max ran ahead of his dad and down the steps to the church basement.

"Wow," he said when he saw the track for the car race. It stretched from one end of the fellowship room to the other end. And the cars. Blue ones, purple ones, and striped ones. Some were designed like old fashioned cars, some were sleek and sporty, and some were made totally from the imagination.

Benny came over to Max. "I like your car," he said. "It looks like it'll go fast."

"As fast as the wind. Let me see yours."

Benny held up a wooden-colored car. It was smooth from sanding, but Max could see it was carved by a knife instead of a power saw.

"How come you didn't paint it?" asked Max.

"The paint was expensive," said Benny. "I'm saving my money though. Next year I'll have paint."

"Yeah," Max said, thinking of the three cans of paint he bought because he couldn't decide if he wanted a green, blue, or red car.

"It's time to get in line to weigh our cars," Benny said. "I walked to the post office three times to weigh mine on the postal scale. It was always just a little too heavy."

Benny's car was weighed first. It weighed exactly five ounces.

Max's car was next.

"Sorry Max," said Mr. Thrill, their club leader. "Your car weighs six ounces. That's one more ounce than you're allowed. Your weights add about a half an ounce apiece. Take off two of them."

"I can't. I mean the weights pull it forward to make it go fast."

"Sorry," said Mr. Thrill. "I see you drilled holes to imbed your weights. They should pop out easy enough."

Max pulled out two weights. He stuck them in his pocket while his car was weighed again.

"4.95 ounces," said Mr. Thrill. "You're all set."

Yeah, set to lose, thought Max.

"I'll be right back," Max said to Mr. Thrill. "I forgot something in my father's car."

Outside, Max pressed the weights back into his derby car. Then he went back inside and waited for his turn.

Max won his first three rounds. So did Benny. Now it was Max's car against Benny's. They stood side by side at the top of the ramp. The gate opened to release the cars. Both cars flew down the wooden track.

"It's a tie," called Mr. Thrill. "Do it again."

The boys ran down to get their cars.

"What makes your car fast?" Max asked Benny.

Benny turned his car over. "See this grove along the bottom? It lets the wind pass through. It's my secret design."

That's a great idea, thought Max. *He deserves to win.*

"What makes your car fast?" Benny asked.

"I, uh, don't know," Max said. "Luck, I guess." Max fingered the weights on the bottom of his car. He wiggled a weight until it came out. There wasn't time to pull out the second weight.

The boys released their cars. Max's car wobbled, hitting the side of the track, slowing it down. Benny's car zipped past the finish line.

"The winner," called Mr. Thrill, holding up Benny's car.

Max thought he'd feel disappointed about losing the trophy, but his heart felt light.

Something to Think About
How do you think Max would have felt if his car won the race?

Something to Read About
Each person should judge his own actions. Then he can be proud for what he himself has done. *Galatians 6:4b*

Something to Pray About
Lord, help me to know the difference between right and wrong. Help me obey you and your law. Amen.

trade fifteen:

Truth

for

Gold

After years of shepherding in the desert, my brother, Moses, didn't expect God to call him to lead the people out of Egypt. But God did, and I joined Moses in going against Pharaoh. Now finally we were free people.

But how were we going to live? We were not used to making decisions. Pharaoh's way was our way of life. Now our direction came from God, but he didn't talk to us every day. Instead he led us through a puffy, white cloud in the daytime and a fiery one at night. It was awesome, but so different from the whips that ruled our lives in Egypt.

We sang and jumped for joy to be free. But after a while desert life got old—hot, dry, dusty. Day after day of the same scene. Finally, God led us to the base of Mt. Sinai. There we at least had a little shade. And we had new hope because Moses was going up Mt. Sinai to meet with God.

The first thundering of God's voice shook everyone in their dusty sandals. Our God who had led us out of Egypt was mighty and powerful! We could hear that. Soon he would send Moses down to tell us how we would become a great nation.

But after a while the days became long and boring. When was Moses coming back?

After days of waiting, the people came to me. "Aaron, when is your brother coming back?"

I didn't know.

"We can't see God, and now we can't see Moses either. We need a god we can see."

They had a point. In Egypt, people worshiped gods they could see—statues and things like the river and the sun. It was a lot easier to believe in a god you could see.

"All right," I said. "I'll make you a little something to help you know that soon we will be living in a land where all the cattle are fat. Bring me your gold."

The Egyptians had given us armloads of gold just to get us to leave Egypt during the last plagues. We had enough gold to make a good-sized golden calf. A calf would remind the people that someday they would be a great nation—just as God promised. They would have plenty of land and cattle.

So I molded the gold into a calf as smooth and shiny as any Egyptian god. The people gushed with praise.

"Yes," they said. "This is the god that brought us out of Egypt."

Finally, I had made the people happy. They trusted me as their leader. But I was a little worried about what I had made. I didn't want them to forget about the Lord, the true God, so I built an altar to him too. "Tomorrow we will have a party," I said. "Bring sacrifices to the Lord."

Like a boy emptying the trash before he can go out to play, they brought their sacrifices to the Lord's altar. Then they worshiped the calf, and the party began. They ate and drank and had fun.

Above the sound of the dancing and noisemaking, I heard a crash. A powdery dust rolled down the mountain. Above it all stood Moses. An angry Moses. He had thrown down the stone tablets with the words of God written on them.

"How did the people talk you into this?" he thundered at me.

My mind rushed for an excuse. "You know how the people get. You were gone so long. And they needed something to worship. I told them to bring me their gold. Then I just threw it into the fire, and this calf came out. It surprised me too. So don't be angry. It just happened."

My story didn't convince Moses. He was angry. "Decide who you will worship," he cried. "The true God or a god made out of gold."

All of us who knew we were wrong in turning away from the true God stood on one side. We lived. The others died.

How could we ever have traded the real God—the God who made the animals and the gold—for a shiny, fat statue?

Something to Think About
Why did the people want a god they could see?

Something to Read About
You can read about Aaron and Moses in Exodus 32.

Something to Pray About
Lord, help us to worship only you. Amen.

trade sixteen:

Flowers *for* Frosting

"I'll take that one and that one," Ean said to the florist as he picked out the biggest and brightest carnations.

"Choose quickly now," said the florist. "I have other customers who want to buy Mother's Day flowers."

"My mother is the best," Ean said. "I don't want any carnations that are small or brown on the edges." Carefully, Ean chose two pink ones to add to the bunch of purple and red.

The carnation perfume went from his nose to his heart.

He emptied his sandwich bag of money on the florist's counter. The florist took every penny except one.

On the way home, Ean met Sam.

"What do you have wrapped in that green paper?" Sam asked.

"Flowers for my mother." Ean peeled back the tissue to show Sam.

"Too bad you didn't buy her bath gel," Sam said. "Almost every mother likes bath gel best. That's what I bought my mother."

"What am I going to do?" Ean asked.

"Don't worry," Sam said. "Because you're my friend, I'll trade the bath gel for the flowers."

Sam took the flowers from Ean, and gave Ean a plastic bottle filled with a thick, pink liquid. Ean took a big whiff. The scent got in his nose and made him sneeze. When Ean could see again, Sam was gone. So Ean started for home again.

A block later, he meet Cindy.

"Are you giving your mother bath gel for Mother's Day?" Cindy asked.

"Yes," said Ean. "Mothers like it the best."

"Not as much as they like cards," Cindy said. "I've seen the mothers on TV. When they get a card, they hug and kiss the person who gave it to them."

"You're right," Ean said.

"I have a card I can give you," Cindy said. "But it's a very expensive card. I'd have to trade it for something. Something like your bath gel."

"Okay," Ean said. He made the trade.

Ean smelled the card. It smelled like school paper. But wasn't Cindy right? Didn't moms like cards the best? So on he walked. Soon he meet Tonia.

"Is that a Mother's Day card?" she asked.

Ean let her hold it.

"It's very plain," Tonia said. "Most mothers like things they can smell."

"So does my mother," Ean said. "What am I going to do? My money is gone."

"Wait here," Tonia said. "I can help you." She took the card and ran into her house. In a few minutes, she came back carrying a small paper cup. A bit of frosting was in the cup. "This frosting smells sweet," she said. "Your mother will like it."

Slowly Ean walked home.

"What's in the cup?" asked Ean's mother.

"It's supposed to be your Mother's Day present," Ean said. "But it isn't what I planned to get for you. I wanted to get you the best thing because you are the best mother." Then he told his mother the whole story.

Mother dipped her finger into the frosting. "Hmm, this is very good frosting. I have an idea."

Ean followed his mother into the kitchen.

"Let's add a little sugar, butter, milk, and vanilla," she said.

They added more and more of the sugar, butter, milk, and vanilla. Soon they had a big bowl of frosting.

"We have enough frosting for a cake," said Ean's mother.

So they baked a big golden cake. Together they covered the cake with frosting.

Ean's mother took a deep breath. "This cake smells so good, I can't wait to have a piece on Mother's Day tomorrow. It'll be the best Mother's Day ever."

Ean hugged his mother. "You're the best mother," he said.

Something to Think About

Did Ean love his mother? How can you tell?

Something to Read About

This is my command: Love each other as I have loved you. *John 15:12*

Something to Pray About

Dear Lord, we give you so little when we give you all our love, but you give us so much when you give us all your love. Amen.

trade seventeen:

A Red Rope *for* Freedom

"Rahab, have you heard the news? The Israelites are camped on the other side of the Jordan River."

My heart drummed. The Israelites! All my life, I had heard stories about these people and their God. Impossible, against-all-odds stories. Why would they be moving so close to my city, the great Jericho? I knew that for years they'd been living in the desert, and I'd often wondered about it. How could *anyone* survive out there? Some people said that these Israelites were still alive because their God fed them.

I filled the table with bowls of fruit, steaming stew, and baskets of bread. My guests sat down to enjoy the daily feast I offered at my inn. I poured dark, red, grape drink into their goblets. "Do you think they'll cross the river?" I asked nervously.

"They may be tempted by our land," said my guest, "but our cities are too strong and our soldiers too many for a bunch of foolish desert bums."

"Don't forget their God took them out of Egypt against the power of the great Pharaoh," I said. "Then he cleared the sea for the Israelites to cross, but drowned all the Egyptians."

"Rahab, that's an old wives' tale. You don't believe it's true, do you?"

After my guests left, I cleared the remains of the meal. I'd never been poor or in need of food, but what if I was someday? Did I have a god like the God of the Israelites to take care of me?

Deep inside me there was an empty place. A place for God. That thought surprised me. I operated my inn for money, for myself. I never let anyone or anything become more important than me. I was successful, so why should I want anything more, especially God.

So much for God. There were more guests at my door.

I opened the door. Two men in rough clothing and dusty sandals stood in my doorway. Israelites!

My hands shook as I poured cool water into their cups. "Your God, is he good to you?"

Their smiles creased the dust in their faces. "He's going to give us all this land. It is our promise from him."

There was no doubt in my mind that what they said was true. I locked the door.

"Come up to the roof with me," I said. "You must hide in case anyone saw you come to my door."

A few minutes later, the door rattled. "Rahab, bring out the men who entered your house. They are spies."

"The men were here," I said, "but they left at sunset so they could get out of the city before the gates closed. Hurry.

If you go quickly, you may catch up to them."

I leaned against the door after I locked it. Then I ran up to the roof.

"It's safe," I called.

The straw pile on my roof moved. Two faces appeared.

"I've heard about your God and the great things he has done," I said to the men. "Could your God show kindness to me and my family when you come into our land?"

"Our lives for your lives!" they said. "If you don't tell anyone about us, we will save you and your family. Hang this red rope in the window of your house. It'll be a sign to our soldiers to save you."

Then they climbed out the back window of my house, scaling the red rope, and ran into the hills for safety. I pulled the red rope back into my house and held it in my hands. *This rope as red as blood will save me,* I thought.

I was ready to trade everything to be on God's side.

Something to Think About
Who did Rahab trust? Why?

Something to Read About
You can read about Rahab in Joshua 2.

Something to Pray About
Lord, thank you for being good to all those who believe in you. Thank you for caring for us always. Amen.

trade eighteen:

The Truth

for

A Good Score

"Renee, here's a green golf ball," said my sister Karla. "Find a golf club your size."

I picked the shortest club I could find. "Thanks for inviting me to play miniature golf with you," I said.

"Mom said if I took my friend Julie, I had to take you," Karla said. "So don't be a bother."

I followed Karla and Julie to the starting point. Eighteen miniature castles stood in the middle of fake green grass.

"Every setup is different," Karla said. "Sometimes you send your ball straight through the castle, and sometimes the hole is inside the castle."

"I'll try," I said.

"Remember, par is two," Julie said. "That means you should get the ball in the hole with two strokes. Of course beginners like you can take six tries."

Karla and Julie went first. Karla tapped her ball into the hole in three easy tries. Julie hit her ball straight to the hole. My ball bounced through the bushes into the castle wall. On my sixth shot, it sputtered in the water surrounding the castle.

It was the same at the second castle. Karla's ball seemed to have eyes for the hole. Julie's ball headed straight for the hole too. But no matter how hard I tried, my ball refused to go where I wanted. While I struggled with my putting, Karla and Julie went ahead to check out the next castle.

At the fifth castle, my ball was only a few feet away from the hole. I knew that on my next try I'd hit it too hard or too soft. So when no one was looking, I tapped the ball with my foot. The ball rolled into the hole.

"What'd you get?" asked Karla when I walked over to them.

"Four," I said.

"Good job, Renee," Julie said.

I decided that from now on I'd take my turn when they weren't watching.

At the tenth hole, I tapped the ball into the hole after six tries. "Two," I told Karla and Julie.

"You're getting better," Karla said.

I really was. No more cheating, I decided.

The next course was an easy shot. I dumped the ball in the hole after five shots. It was the best I'd done.

"Five," I shouted.

"I thought you were getting better," Karla said. "That's not very good for that hole."

"Guess I went too fast," I mumbled.

On the eighteenth hole, I slammed the ball with my club. The ball zoomed over the green and smacked into a sign across the way. As I picked up my ball, I read the sign. *Cheater's only get better at cheating—Not better at the game.* I looked around. Was someone watching me or something?

I looked over to where the ball was *supposed* to be and shook my head. I'd never make it into the hole in under six shots. But as I moved my foot in place to try my "secret" method of putting, I remembered the sign. Maybe they had a point. Besides, the more I lied to Karla and Julie, the worse I felt.

So this time, while Karla and Julie watched impatiently, I did it the hard way—one stroke at a time. After six strokes the ball dribbled into the hole. Suddenly bells rang and sirens screamed. The owner came running over to me.

"Congratulations, you've won a free game," he said. "Your ball was number one thousand to drop into this hole."

Karla, Julie, and everyone in the miniature golf park clapped.

"The last time we had a thousand-ball winner, he hit a hole in one," said the owner. "Was it a hole in one for you too?"

"No," I whispered. "It was a six."

The manager dug into his pocket. "You're the first person who hasn't claimed a hole in one on this deal. For your honesty, I'm giving you *two* extra game tickets," he said smiling.

As we headed back to the beginning to play another round, I was smiling too. And this time when I yelled out "four" for hole one, it was the truth.

Something to Think About
How do you think Renee felt when she lied about her scores?

Something to Read About
Lord, who may enter your Holy Tent? Who may live on your holy mountain? Only those who are innocent and who do what is right. Such people speak the truth from their hearts and do not tell lies about others. *Psalm 15: 1-3*

Something to Pray About
Jesus, sometimes lies seem so easy. Help us to remember that you want us to tell the truth always—even when it makes us look bad. Amen.

trade nineteen:

shouts
for
swords

The wheat dust burned in my eyes. My skin itched, but it was useless scratching. Beating seeds out of grains of wheat created a dust that settled in every thread of my clothes. Of course, doing this job in a pit made matters worse. Any good farmer would use the wind to work with him. But I knew that if I was going to have any flour for my family, I had to work secretly in a pit.

For the past seven years, our enemies, the Midianites, had watched us grow our wheat to a golden color under the blue skies. Then, when we harvested the grain, they came and took it. This year I wanted to make sure that didn't happen.

I wiped the sweat off my forehead. "Lord, when are you going to rescue your people?" I wondered aloud.

Something rustled above my head. The wind? No, it was an angel!

"Gideon, you are a strong, young man," the angel said. "The Lord is with you and knows the troubles of the Israelites."

"If that's true, where are all the wonders of the Lord who brought the people out of Egypt?"

The angel turned toward me. "Go in the Lord's strength and save Israel from Midian."

"Me? Not me. My family is weak, and I'm the least important person in my family."

The angel answered. "The Lord will be with you and will strike down the Midianites."

Was he serious? "I'm going to gather some meat and bread for an offering to the Lord," I told him. When I returned, I said, "If what you have told me is true, give me a sign."

Suddenly, my offering of bread and meat was on fire. It was gone in an instant!

I knew then that I had really been talking to God's angel. So I built an altar to worship God.

My altar pleased God. What didn't please him were all the altars in our land to the gods of our wicked neighbors. No wonder God allowed the Midianites to harm us. So later that day, after it was dark, I went out with some of my friends and destroyed the places where the people worshiped the pretend god Baal.

In the morning, the men of the village went to my father. "Give us your son. We want to kill him. He destroyed our altars to Baal."

"If Baal is your great god, let Baal fight for himself," my father said.

When the people agreed, I was sure I was safe. A pretend god couldn't harm me!

I knew it was time to lead the fight against Midian. So I took my trumpet and traveled through many villages. Many men were eager to join me to take a stand against our enemies. But were there enough of us to fight against the great army of the Midianites?

When I thought about it, my skinny legs shook all the way down to my sandals. Hiding in my pit and threshing wheat was safer than leading an army against the Midianites.

"Lord, I need another sign," I said. I dug my fingers deep into the oily wool of a sheepskin. "Make this wool wet with dew in the morning. But keep the ground dry."

God did it!

Well, maybe that was too easy, I thought. *The wool is always the first thing to attract moisture.* So the next day, I asked God to make the ground wet and the wool dry.

God did it! And then I knew for sure that I could trust God and that I didn't have to be afraid.

So early the next morning, I called my army. "Too many," the Lord said, as if I was a schoolboy inviting the entire school over for a birthday party. "Send home all those who are afraid. I don't want anyone to boast they won this battle with their strength."

I had been proud of enlisting thirty-two thousand men. Now I had only ten thousand men left.

"Still too many," the Lord said. "Take them down to the river to drink. There I'll tell you which ones will go with you."

At the river God chose only three hundred men! I had traded a decent-sized army for a small but brave gang.

That night as we edged around the Midianite camp, it looked as if even their camels outnumbered us. And our swords—well, we had traded them for trumpets, clay jars, and torches. We were going to battle with no battle equipment.

As the Midianite guards changed stations in the valley, we surrounded their camp. I flashed my signal. Then we blasted our noisy ram's horns, broke our jars, and twirled our lights, tumbling into their camp.

We fought the Midianites that night—and won! It seemed as if there was an army behind each trumpeter. And I guess there was, because God was behind each one of my men. I had traded human power for God's power!

Something to Think About
How was it possible for Gideon's small army to win the battle?

Something to Read About
You can read about Gideon in Judges 6 and 7.

Something to Pray About
Dear Lord, sometimes we feel alone and afraid. Help us to know you are always with us. Amen.

trade twenty:

Ten Newspapers *for* A New Truck

"Murry, come back here. Murry! Murry!"

I chased after my big-footed, hairy Saint Bernard.

Murry ran with Mr. Taff's newspaper in his big, wet mouth. I followed him around the corner and up the hill to the ice-cream store.

At the ice-cream store, Murry dropped the newspaper. He swept his tail against the sidewalk in front of a big, cardboard ice-cream cone.

"No ice cream today," I said picking up the newspaper. "How can I make you understand that the ice-cream coupon was only in last week's paper?"

I tossed the wet, chewed-up newspaper behind the bushes. It landed on top of nine other soggy newspapers with a thud. My heart went thud too.

"Mr. Taff is going to be upset about his missing newspaper," I said to Murry. "Every day I tell him, 'I'll find the newspaper thief and make him stop.' Today I'll have to tell him you're the thief, Murry, because I can't make you stop."

Slowly, we walked down the hill, around the corner, and past Mr. Taff's house.

"Stop, Allison," called Mr. Taff. "The newspaper thief came again this morning. Did you see him?"

"Yes, Mr. Taff, I saw him. And it's a dog."

"A dog!" said Mr. Taff. "Well, we'll have to catch that dog and send him to the dog pound."

"What happens to dogs at the pound?" I asked.

"They're locked up in a cage so they can't cause trouble," said Mr. Taff.

"I'll find the dog and tell him to stop taking your newspaper," I said.

I waved goodbye to Mr. Taff. "Come on, Murry. Time to go home." Murry sat on top of Mr. Taff's sprinkler and didn't move. Finally, I tugged at Murry's collar and dragged him home.

The next morning, I tied Murry's leash to the porch railing. But when the newspaper clunked on Mr. Taff's driveway, Murry broke loose from the leash. He bounded out of the yard, ran into Mr. Taff's driveway, and picked up the newspaper.

"Drop it," I called.

But Murry ran. He ran around the corner and up the hill to the ice-cream store. He didn't drop the paper until I stopped beside him outside the ice-cream store door.

I picked up the wet, ragged newspaper. "No more hiding the evidence behind the bushes," I said to Murry. "It's time to tell Mr. Taff the truth."

Down the hill and around the corner, I marched with Murry beside me.

"Have you found the thief, Allison?" asked Mr. Taff.

"Yes," I said. "It's me."

"You?" asked Mr. Taff. "Not a dog?"

"Murry picked up the paper, but I taught him to do it the first time. So you can't blame him. So make me buy you a new paper every day, but don't put Murry in the pound."

"I didn't think you could teach Murry anything," said Mr. Taff.

"You're sort of right about that," I said. "It must have been the ice cream. Last week I stole your paper to get an extra ice-cream coupon. Then Murry and I went to the ice-cream store. The next day and every day since then, Murry has gone into your yard. He takes the newspaper and goes to the ice-cream store."

"Why didn't you tell me this earlier?" asked Mr. Taff.

"At first I thought I could stop Murry, and you'd forget about a few missing papers. Then I decided to tell on Murry. But I knew it wouldn't be fair to blame him for something that I taught him."

Mr. Taff smiled. "Because you were brave and did the right thing," he said, "I'll make you a trade. If you can teach Murry to bring the newspaper from the driveway to my front steps, I'll forget about the stolen newspapers."

I knew just how to do it! After two dishes of ice cream, Murry learned what to do with Mr. Taff's newspaper.

I learned something too. Believe me, it's never worth stealing for an extra scoop of ice cream—especially if you have a dog named Murray!

Something to Think About

Why did Allison decide to tell Mr. Taff the truth?

Something to Read About

Read 1 Kings 3:16-28, the story about a powerful king who trusted God to help him make the right decisions.

Something to Pray About

Dear Lord, it's often easier to choose wrong instead of right. Give us courage to always choose the right. Amen.

trade twenty-one:

My Homeland

for

A Stranger's Field

for

A Home

It was a trade I wanted to make. But it wasn't one that would make me rich or famous.

"Ruth, don't give up your homeland. Stay and find a new husband," said my mother-in-law, Naomi.

Instead of listening to her practical words, I clung to her. Naomi had moved to my country with her husband and two sons when their land near Bethlehem dried up after years without rain.

I noticed right away that Naomi's family was different than most people in my town. And I soon figured out that it had something to do with the God they worshiped.

Before long I had the chance to find out more about that God. I married one of Naomi's sons. My friend Orpah married my husband's brother.

We were happy for a few years. But then my father-in-law, Naomi's husband, died, and soon my husband and his brother also died. Naomi, Orpah, and I cried for ourselves and each other. Joy fled every corner of our home.

Then came the news that food was growing in Bethlehem. A spark of hope came back to Naomi's sad eyes.

"I will go with you," I said.

"No," she said. "You'll have a better life if you stay here."

She was right. If I went with her, I'd probably never marry again. I'd be a widow forever, always struggling to provide food for Naomi and myself. But at least I'd be able to worship the God I loved—the God of Israel.

"I will go where you go," I told Naomi. "Your people will be my people, and your God will be my God."

The fields were ripe with grain when we left. There would certainly be a big harvest in Moab this year. Would there be plenty of food in Bethlehem too?

We crossed the Jordan River and traveled through a hot desert until we came to the grassy hills of Judah. Below us, Naomi pointed out the small town of Bethlehem. In the fields surrounding it, stalks of grain blew like golden waves.

"Thank you, Lord," I whispered. "You haven't sent us here on false hope."

Before long I learned that God commanded land owners to permit the poor to pick up grain that had fallen in the fields. So early the next morning I went to a field. The men swung curved knives, cutting down bundles of barley. Quickly the women followed them, tying up the bundles. Sometimes a stalk or two didn't get in a bundle. If it fell to the ground, poor people like me were allowed to take it.

I worked hard all morning. Some of the other poor people took long breaks under the shade of dark, thick, green leaves, but I wanted to make sure I had enough food for two.

The other workers talked about the owner of the field. They called him Boaz as if he was their best friend. I tried not to listen. It made the emptiness of not having a friend even greater.

Later in the day, Boaz came to check on the harvest. As he talked with the foreman, they were looking directly at me. What were they saying?

Then Boaz walked into the field, heading right in my direction. I nearly dropped the fine strands of barley stalks I had gathered so carefully.

"Ruth, I'm glad you are here," Boaz said. "Don't gather grain in any other fields. And whenever you're thirsty, get a drink from the water jars."

That was the beginning of a wonderful friendship. In fact, after Boaz and I got to know each other better, we got married.

When our first baby was born, tears of joy glistened in Naomi's eyes. She rocked our son lovingly, as if he were her own grandchild. God had changed her sadness into joy!

So I may have traded my homeland for a stranger's field, but God traded it again and gave me a home filled with love. That's the kind of God I now belong to!

Something to Think About
Why did God give Ruth so much?

Something to Read About
You can read Ruth's story in the book of Ruth.

Something to Pray About
Lord of all joy, thank you for bringing a son into Ruth and Naomi's life. Thank you for your Son, Jesus Christ, who brought joy to all of our lives. Amen.

trade twenty-two:

A Big Bed *for* A Lumpy Bed

It was a warm summer afternoon. Roseline was packing her suitcase. She put all her night things on one side of the suitcase and all her day things on the other side.

"Are you ready?" asked her mother.

"Almost," said Roseline. "Is staying overnight at Grandma's a very grown-up thing to do?"

"I think so," her mother said. "Last year you were afraid to go away overnight, but this time you want to go. That must mean you are more grown-up than last year."

"Maybe I should take my bunny dishes to Grandma's."

"No," said Mother. "Grandma has special dishes."

"What about cookies?"

"No," said Mother. "Grandma will have snacks."

"I could bring my yellow blanket. Grandma might not have enough blankets for company."

"Yes," said Mother. "Maybe Grandma doesn't have enough blankets."

Roseline rolled up her favorite blanket. It didn't fit into the suitcase. She took out all her night clothes and her day clothes. The blanket still didn't fit.

"Do you want another suitcase?" asked Mother.

"No," said Roseline. "If I go to Grandma's with two suitcases, she'll think I'm staying for two nights. I'll leave the blanket home. I'm very grown-up now. I can sleep without my special blanket."

At Grandma's house, it was very quiet.

"Do you have any storybooks?" asked Roseline.

"No," said Grandma, "but I have a very good story in my head. I'll tell it to you."

Roseline snuggled against Grandma, and the story began. It was a story about Roseline's mother when she was a girl about the same size as Roseline.

At supper time, Grandma set flowered plates on the table. She put shiny poached eggs and toast with orange marmalade on the flowered plates. Roseline had never eaten off flowered plates, and she had never eaten poached eggs for supper. But she decided it was a very grown-up thing to do, so she ate her eggs and toast.

At bedtime, Grandma showed Roseline where to put her things in the guest room.

"This is a soft bed," said Grandma. "I'd let you sleep in your mother's old bed in the room across the hall, but that bed has lumps in it."

Grandma kissed Roseline goodnight.

Roseline took her nightgown out of the suitcase. She put her clothes for the next day in the dresser drawer. The room was very grown-up. The wallpaper had wide blue stripes, and the curtains were long and heavy. She put on her nightgown and crawled underneath the silky blue comforter.

This bed is very big, thought Roseline. *Three Roselines could fit into this bed.*

She couldn't sleep. So she put on the light. There were books on a shelf next to the window—fat books with no pictures.

Maybe there's a storybook in my mother's room, she thought.

Tiptoeing across the hall, she opened the door to her mother's old room. The walls were papered with soft, yellow flowers. The short, skinny bed had a fuzzy white bedspread. Roseline pulled back the bedspread and stretched out. The bed squeaked, and a lump popped up right in the middle of her back. It wasn't one bit comfortable.

Roseline got out of the lumpy bed. On the night stand was a white Bible. She opened the front cover. Inside were the words: *To my daughter, Caroline. Jesus sends his angels to watch over you.*

Roseline remembered that Caroline was her mother's name. She crawled back into the lumpy bed. It felt just right to sleep in. Roseline closed her eyes, thinking about Jesus sending his angels to watch over her just like he did when her mother was a little girl sleeping in this bed.

Something to Think About

Why did thinking about the angels help Roseline go to sleep?

Something to Read About

He has put his angels in charge of you. They will watch over you wherever you go. *Psalm 91:11*

Something to Pray About

Dear Lord, keep us in your care. May we never be afraid. Amen.

trade twenty-three:

A Stab for A Snip

Every day was a game of hide-and-seek. As the sun set over the hillsides, dark shapes swallowed me, but I couldn't go home. I couldn't go back into the city. I knew that if one of King Saul's men spotted me, they'd be after me again.

King Saul had been chosen by God, and I wanted to serve him, but the more battles I won, the more the people cheered me instead of King Saul. People danced in the streets, singing, "Hurray for David. Saul has killed thousands of enemies, but David has killed tens of thousands."

Saul's jealousy grew into hatred. His solution to my growing popularity was to get rid of me.

If it wasn't for the Lord, even a forest of trees or a mountainside of giant boulders couldn't have hid me from Saul and his men. His traps, spies, and messengers were everywhere.

But God was with me, and I knew he wanted me to continue to help his people. So whenever I heard about a village that needed help because of the Philistines, I came out of hiding. One day, word came to me about a small town near the Philistine border. The Philistines had stormed into this village with their iron swords. The villagers hid in fear while the Philistines swept through barns and houses, taking everything they could carry. In a matter of hours, harvests of food and grain that the Israelites had worked for all year were stolen by the Philistines.

It wasn't fair to the people. I had to fight.

My men and I crept into the little town. Philistine soldiers with weapons were everywhere. Fighting against them was like going against a monster with iron teeth. My hands were powerful enough to wrestle with a bear, but the cutting power of the Philistine weapons was beyond the flesh and muscle of my hands.

I asked the Lord for advice. He said, "Go. I'll give the Philistines to you."

As always, God's word was trustworthy. We won the battle against the Philistine army. But someone leaked word to Saul about what I'd done. Now Saul knew where to find me.

Back to hide-and-seek. My men and I ran, moving from place to place. My face and arms were burnt from days in the hot sun. We climbed sideways along a mountainside like wild goats until we found a cave and crawled inside. We knew we'd probably be sharing our dark, damp camp with a few creatures, but it'd give us a break from running and darting like brown leaves in the wind.

Suddenly the entrance to the cave was darkened by a figure. A large animal? No, it was King Saul himself, but he couldn't see us.

My men whispered to me. "Sneak up on him. Kill him. The Lord is giving him to you."

In the darkness of the cave, I slipped up behind him. Every advantage was mine. I knew the exact fit of his armor against his body. I drew my sword, reached for the bottom of his robe, and snipped off the corner. Moving back into the dark corners of the cave, I waited until he left.

"David, how could you trade a perfect opportunity to kill Saul for snipping off a piece of his garment?" asked one of my men. "If Saul was dead, you'd be king."

"The king is God's chosen leader," I said. "When God is ready to put an end to Saul's life, he'll do it."

I ran out of the cave.

"My Lord, the king!" I called, holding up the piece of Saul's robe. "I could've taken your life, but I didn't."

Saul cried when he realized that I had spared him. He promised to stop chasing me. He went home. And I went back to my hiding place. Saul's promises couldn't be trusted, but I knew I'd never trade his life for an opportunity to become king. It was up to God to choose the time to trade Saul's kingdom for mine.

Something to Think About

Was David tempted to kill Saul in the cave?

Something to Read About

You can read about David and Saul in 1 Samuel 24.

Something to Pray About

Dear Lord, keep us from hurting others. Help us to wait for you to make all things fair and just. Amen.

trade twenty-four:

The Truth
for
A Good Time

Even though Bram Burket was in the fifth grade, he noticed me in the hallways at school. Sometimes his punches stung all the way to my bones, but fifth graders didn't even see most third graders, so I felt honored.

"Hey, kid," Bram shouted to me on Friday after school. "Are you going to the hot-air balloon races on Saturday?"

"Yep. I've even saved enough money for a tethered ride."

"How much is that?" he asked.

"Twelve dollars." Just saying that amount made my fingers tingle. I'd been saving for two months.

"If you come with me," Bram said, "I'd get you a deal. You'd have at least two dollars left over for a funnel cake."

"Wow." My mouth watered for a piping-hot funnel cake dusted with powered sugar.

"Here's the deal," Bram said. "We'll put our money together and get a discount on the second ride. We'll split the money we save."

"Are you sure?" I asked. "I've never seen discounts on tethered balloon rides."

"Trust me," said Bram. "Don't you think I know what I'm doing?"

Bram always knew what he was doing. He was a great guy. My hero.

"This is the way we'll do it," Bram said. "You give me your money. I'll put it with mine."

I ran into my house. Twelve one-dollar bills were rolled into a wad inside my pillowcase.

Bram was waiting for me on my porch steps. It was a proud moment handing my money over to Bram. We were partners.

"Meet me here tomorrow morning," Bram said. "Seven o'clock sharp. Don't be late."

That night, I had a dream. In my dream, Bram introduced me as his buddy. We first rode in a huge purple balloon shaped like the favorite dinosaur of my younger friends.

In the morning, I waited on the porch steps. Quarter after seven. Where was Bram? The sky was filled with splashes of color. If he didn't hurry, we'd miss our tethered ride and lift-off of all the other balloons. I tapped my foot faster with each new balloon that lifted its silky purples, reds, oranges, and yellows up into the blue sky. My stomach growled. Eight o'clock. Something felt very wrong. Was Bram sick in bed?

I ran to his house and knocked on his door.

"Bram isn't here," his mother said. "He left two hours ago."

I nodded, but my stomach felt sick. My hero was a liar. I'd find him and make him confess.

At the park, a group of fifth graders carried someone on their shoulders.

"Bram, Bram! Bram the brave!" shouted one of Bram's buddies.

"What do you mean, Bram the brave?" I shouted.

"A gust of wind threw the gondola off balance," said a fifth grader. "The tethers could've snapped, but Bram pulled the rip cord and landed the balloon safely."

"Why didn't the pilot do it?" I asked.

"He was pulling a little girl back into the gondola. When the wind tipped the gondola, she almost fell over the edge."

Bram scrambled down from his place of honor. "Philip, I uh..."

All the bad names I wanted to call Bram shouted in my head. Even if he was a hero, he wasn't *my* hero. Not anymore. I opened my mouth to speak. Then I noticed how pale Bram's face was. I thought about how bad he would feel if I told his friends what he had done with my money.

"Most people would have been too afraid to think of pulling the rip cord," I said.

"Let's go," said one of Bram's buddies. "The Snoopy balloon is being inflated."

"You guys go ahead," said Bram. "I have something to take care of with Philip."

Bram twisted his cap in his hands. "I'm sorry, kid," he said. "I shouldn't have used your money for the ride."

I nodded.

"Why didn't you squeal on me in front of the guys?" he asked.

"You were a hero to them," I said.

"A real hero would've saved his own money for a ride," said Bram.

I nodded again.

Two months later I found the money in an envelope with my name on it that Bram had stuck in my desk. "Thanks a lot, kid," the note said. "Sorry it took so long to pay you back. Sorry for everything else too."

I smiled and tucked the money in my pocket. I knew the balloons would be back next summer, and I would be ready.

Something to Think About
Was it easy for Philip to forgive Bram?

Something to Read About
Forgive each other just as God forgave you in Christ. *Ephesians 4:32b*

Something to Pray About
Lord, help us to forgive others even when they don't deserve it. Thank you for always forgiving us. Amen.

trade twenty-five:

silver
for
spectacular wisdom

In our nation no one was honored more than my dad, King David. Throughout the cities and countryside, people loved him. And you couldn't blame them. For the first time since our people had come to the promised land, we were free from enemies. King David had driven away the Philistines who had stolen from us for years. Now all the Caananite people were under my father's rule.

Dad didn't ask the people to sing praises to him, though. Instead he wrote praises for the people to sing to God.

I loved the words he wrote. I fingered the shapes of the letters. The smell of ink on sheepskin was my father's fragrance.

"Listen to this, Solomon," he would say.

And when I closed my eyes, I could hear the voice of God like thunder. I could sense the lovingkindness of God like the spring rain.

Then Dad would hold me close, telling me how God loved me like a father.

When my father wasn't working on his writing, he was busy drawing and writing down figures.

"What are you doing, Father?" I asked.

"It's a dream I've had for a long time." He unrolled a wide scroll. "What do you think?"

I gasped. Even though the sketches were rough, I could see the plan for a wonderful building.

"It's a temple for God," Father said. "It has been almost five hundred years since Moses led the people out of Egypt. All this time, we've had only a tent for worship. Now that the promised land is completely ours, I want to build him a beautiful temple."

It was such a wonderful plan that I was sure God would give my father many more years of health and strength so that he could start building.

But no matter how many plans my father drew, God said no to him about building the temple. God said my father, King David, had fought too many battles. The blood of too many people was on his hands.

Finally the days of my father's strength were gone. He was too weak to get up in the morning. He shivered in his bed. The servants covered him with blankets, but even that wasn't enough to keep him warm.

"Solomon," he said to me. "You'll be the new king. God has chosen you because of your heart. God knows you love him. So when I die and you sit on the throne, God wants *you* to build the temple."

And that's just what I did. When the throne was mine, the work on the temple began. During the day, I ordered supplies and checked over the plans. At night, the plans danced in my head. As I dreamed about carvings for the walls, God came to me.

"Ask whatever you want from me," said the Lord, "and I will give it to you."

"Lord, you have given me a big responsibility in taking over my father's kingdom. Give me a wise heart to rule over the people. Help me to know right from wrong. No one can rule over your people without your help."

I wouldn't have traded God's gift of wisdom for all the gold and riches in the world. For my task of building God's temple, I needed the wisdom of an engineer, a plumber, a carpenter, an artist, and a banker. I needed the wisdom to know how to use billions of dollars worth of gold, silver, bronze, precious stones, and cedar wood.

Finally my work was complete. In God's beautiful, holy temple we sang the songs my father wrote to worship our heavenly Father.

God filled my heart, soul, and mind with so many things that, like my father, I began writing. I wrote about God's wisdom that I saw through the plants, birds, and animals. In all of creation, I saw God's love and care.

Our God is wonderful, isn't he?

Something to Think About
Why was Solomon so wise?

Something to Read About
You can read about Solomon in 1 Kings 2 and 3.

Something to Pray About
Dear Lord, your beauty and glory shine brighter than gold or jewels. You are more wonderful than palaces or riches. May we always put you first. Amen.

trade twenty-six:
A Check
for
A Treasure

Leslie's house was built with bricks and wood. Two other houses on her block were almost the same as hers. But there was something very, very special about Leslie's house. Five steps down from the family room and behind the garage, Leslie's father had added an apartment. It was an apartment for Leslie's grandpa.

The first thing Leslie did each day after school was visit her grandpa.

And the first thing Grandpa did when Leslie knocked on the apartment door was a secret.

"Are you ready for me?" Leslie would ask.

"Almost," Grandpa would call back.

The door was never locked, but Leslie always waited for Grandpa to call "ready" before she opened the door and let herself inside.

Leslie put her ear against the door. She could hear Grandpa's wheelchair bumping against the bed, then the dresser.

"Ready!" called Grandpa.

Leslie opened the door and headed straight for the chair next to Grandpa's wheelchair.

"Look at this," said Grandpa. "I found a shiny quarter. What are we going to do with it?"

Leslie laughed with Grandpa, putting the shiny quarter in the big glass jar with all the other shiny quarters. The quarter landed with a dull thud on the top.

"Grandpa, you can't keep it a secret anymore," said Leslie. "I know where you get your quarters. I heard the wheelchair bump against the dresser today. The quarters are in the dresser, right?"

"Could be," said Grandpa. "But quarters come from banks, not dressers. Do you think I could walk to the bank?"

Leslie pushed Grandpa's wheelchair over to the kitchenette. Grandpa turned on the burner underneath the teakettle. Leslie took the cookie tin off the shelf.

"I know you couldn't walk to the bank, Grandpa, but quarters don't appear like magic every time I knock on your door. I used to believe that when I was little but not anymore."

"Does that mean you won't be knocking on my door again?" asked Grandpa.

Leslie laughed. "Of course not, Grandpa. I'll be here every day knocking on your door. I come because I like your stories and your cookies— and you!"

Grandpa's thin lips smiled under his heavy, white mustache. "Every visit has been worth more to me than a jarful of quarters. But we're going to have to do something about those quarters. The jar doesn't have room for any more."

Leslie nibbled on a cookie. Were Grandpa's quarters gone? Was the quarter game over?

Suddenly the bright spot of sun in Grandpa's window was gone.

"Read the verse from the calendar today," Grandpa said.

Leslie read, "Luke 12:34. Your heart will be where your treasure is."

Grandpa's eyes closed. Leslie quietly left the room.

The next day when Leslie knocked on the door, Grandpa said "ready" without telling Leslie to wait. Leslie's gaze went straight to the place where the jar usually rested. It was gone. Grandpa held an envelope. He gave it to Leslie.

"Open it," said Grandpa.

A check for two hundred dollars written to Leslie Sullivan fell out of the envelope.

"The money from the quarters," Grandpa said. "I thought you could buy one of those electronic games. I know that's what all your friends do after school."

Leslie gave Grandpa a hug and ran out with the check.

For two days after school, Leslie didn't visit Grandpa. The first day she went to the bank with her mom. The second day she went to the store.

"Are you sure this is what you want?" asked her mother.

"I stayed awake all night last night deciding," said Leslie.

On the third day, Leslie knocked on Grandpa's door.

"Who's there?" asked Grandpa.

"You're supposed to say 'ready,'" said Leslie.

Grandpa called "ready." And Leslie walked into the room with the glass jar she bought at the store. She set the jar on the table and dropped a quarter in the top.

"What's this?" asked Grandpa.

"I traded the check you gave me back into quarters. I want to spend more days with you—a whole new jarful of days!" Leslie said.

Something to Think About
What do you think Leslie liked best about her visits with Grandpa?

Something to Read About
Your heart will be where your treasure is. *Luke 12:34*

Something to Pray About
Dear Lord, thank you for loving us and for giving us people to love. Amen.

trade twenty-seven:

Her Baby *for* Mine

It was a morning I'll never forget. Sunbeams warmed up my small apartment when I first awoke. But something was missing. Usually my baby's cries woke me much earlier than this. *He must be sleepy,* I thought to myself.

I could hear the sounds of my roommate moving around in the apartment. Like me, she had a small baby. And I assumed she was busy with him.

I rolled over to check on my small son. "Wake up, sleepyhead," I said with a smile.

But my baby didn't move. I picked him up in my arms, but he still didn't move. And then I knew. He wasn't sleepy—he was dead.

I sat there in my room crying quietly for a long time. How could such a terrible thing have happened? Did I roll over on him while I was sleeping? I took his small hand in mine, thinking about how I had loved to play with his long fingers and toes while he nursed.

And that's when I noticed. This baby didn't have long, slender fingers. He had short, fat fingers. I opened his blanket and studied his face. This wasn't my baby—it was my roommate's baby!

I hurried into the next room where my roommate sat rocking a baby in the far, dark corner. The baby cried and waved his hands. Hands with long, slender fingers.

She must have traded babies with me!

"Let me see your baby," I said.

She wrapped a stained blanket tightly around the baby. The baby cried harder.

"You have *my* baby," I said.

"You can't prove it," she said. "You just want this baby because it's living and yours is dead."

I wanted to scream at her and take my baby out of her arms, but I didn't want to frighten him. So gently, I spoke to her. "Please, you'll never be happy with a son that truly isn't yours." The baby quieted at the sound of my voice. He reached out his arms toward me, but my roommate pulled him away.

We argued back and forth. Finally, I said, "Let the king decide. Everyone says the king is wiser than any man."

"That's fine," she said, "but it's my word against yours."

She was right, but maybe the king could see through our words. Maybe he could see I was telling the truth.

My roommate held her head high all the way to the palace. After all, she had the baby in her arms. So she was sure the king would believe she was the baby's mother.

As we stood before King Solomon explaining our story, I didn't even think about the awesome fact that we were in the king's palace. All I thought about was getting my baby back.

Suddenly I was aware of what the king was ordering his servants to do.

"Cut the baby in half. Give each woman a share."

Someone was coming toward my baby with a sword.

"No!" I shouted. "Let the baby live. She can keep the baby." I was so frightened for my baby that I almost fainted. This king wasn't so wise after all. He nearly killed my baby.

Then King Solomon took the baby out of my roommate's arms and brought him to me. "I know the baby is yours," he said. "Only the true mother would care if the baby lived or died."

My son reached his slender fingers up to my face. I felt his touch as I looked into the king's face.

Now I knew what made the great King Solomon so wise. He understood the love of a mother! I was sure his wisdom came from God.

Something to Think About
How could the mother tell that King Solomon was really wise?

Something to Read About
You can read about Solomon's great wisdom and wealth in 1 Kings 3, 4, and 10.

Something to Pray About
Dear Lord, you are our king. When we rush to you with our problems, you welcome us into your presence. And in your great love and wisdom, you care for us each and every day. Thank you. Amen.

trade twenty-eight:

A Guinea Pig
for
A Chance To Care

"The baby guinea pigs are fighting," Abby told her teacher, Mrs. Robbins.

"Having two male guinea pigs in the same cage doesn't always work," Mrs. Robbins said. "What do you think we should do, Abby?"

"Someone from the class could adopt one of the guinea pigs," Abby said.

"Someone like me. My brother has an empty cage at home. He has food pellets from his rabbits too."

Mrs. Robbins smiled. "I'd trust you to take good care of a guinea pig, but first we should give an equal chance to the rest of the class."

Abby pulled a paper towel roll out of her backpack. Carrot sticks wrapped in plastic wrap slipped out of the long tube. She put the paper towel roll in the cage; both guinea pigs tugged at it.

"Look," Ginger said, "they're playing tug-of-war."

The guinea pigs chewed the cardboard until they were standing nose to nose. Then Harry, the black pig, nipped Silvester, the brown pig.

"Stop," Abby said. She dropped carrots in front on them. "Chew on these."

Harry finished his carrot. Then he bit into Silvester's carrot, and their fighting began again.

"Would anyone besides Abby like to take care of Silvester at home?" asked Mrs. Robbins.

Ginger and Tony raised their hands.

"Thank you," said Mrs. Robbins. "Write a paragraph telling me why you'd like to take care of Silvester. The person who does the best job of convincing me can take Silvester home."

Tony sat right down at his desk and started to write.

Ginger stroked Silvester's silky brown hair. "Silvester," she whispered, "I wish you could come home with me." She sat down at her desk and started writing too.

Abby dumped the rest of her carrots in the cage. Didn't Mrs. Robbins notice that she brought carrots every day? And she was the one who changed their water too.

Abby sharpened her pencil three times and used up five pieces of paper before she turned her paragraph in to Mrs. Robbins. "Please let it be me," she prayed.

After the last recess, Mrs. Robbins said, "It was hard to choose between Ginger and Abby. Finally, I had to choose Abby because she has all the supplies to take care of Silvester."

Abby turned toward Ginger, pointing her finger at herself. "Mine," she whispered.

Ginger squeezed her eyes shut.

Tony raised his hand. "What's wrong with my reason?"

"When I read that you wanted another pet so you'd have an even dozen, I thought you already had enough pets," Mrs. Robbins said with a smile.

Abby looked at Ginger again. Her eyes were still shut. Tears leaked through her closed eyelids.

"What did Ginger write?" Abby asked.

"Ginger, may I read your paragraph to everyone?" asked Mrs. Robbins.

Ginger nodded.

"Dear Mrs. Robbins, I have a younger brother who goes to a special school because he cannot walk and talk. You wouldn't think so, but he's very smart. Some afternoons when everyone plays outside he gets lonely. I think Silvester would be a good friend for him. I know this is just a wish because we don't have a cage or food for Silvester. We don't have money for it either. But even if you can't send Silvester home with me, please wish for something good for my brother. Ginger.

Silvester and Harry chased each other and squealed. The rest of the class was quiet.

Tony raised his hand. "I want to wish something good for Ginger's brother too," he said.

"I think we all do," said Mrs. Robbins. "We could make it a class project."

Abby hid behind her social studies book.

Mrs. Robbins wrote everyone's ideas on the chalkboard. Abby peeked at the list:

- Send cards
- Buy a pass to the zoo
- Make a funny video

Abby looked at Silvester. She'd love to bring him home. Then she looked at Ginger and thought about her brother.

Abby raised her hand high. "How about a Saturday morning pancake breakfast at school?" she said. "With the money we raise, we could buy a cage for Silvester. Then Ginger could take him home to her brother."

Ginger raised her hand. "My brother loves pancakes. He'd come too!"

One person clapped. Then everyone clapped.

"A pancake breakfast it is," said Mrs. Robbins. "Silvester and Harry will just have to get along with each other for a few more days."

Something to Think About
Why did Abby decide to help Ginger bring Silvester home?

Something to Read About
Do not be interested only in your own life, but be interested in the lives of others. *Philippians 2:4*

Something to Pray About
Lord, open our eyes so that we see what others need. Amen.

trade twenty-nine:

A Meal *for* A Promise

There was no escape from the heat. It breathed from the ground and melted down from the sky. The first thing people said to each other was, "Can you believe this weather?" No one could remember a year as hot and dry as this one.

For me it was more than hot and dry; it was scary. My husband was dead. It was up to me to provide for my son. Could I manage when food was so scarce?

"Worship Baal," my neighbor said. "He's a god who brings good life to earth."

That was crazy. People everywhere were calling to Baal. And it didn't seem to make one bit of difference. No, there had to be someone greater than Baal.

I heard from someone that the God of Israel was causing this burning heat with no rain as a punishment for his people who were turning away from him. Could that be true? If so, all this pleading to Baal was like throwing words into a hole in the ground.

"Mama," called my son. "When will we bake the bread for our supper?"

"Soon." I patted his thin shoulders.

I wanted to wait just a little longer because this would be our last meal. If I went begging, I'd only hear those same words again—"Worship Baal."

"Mama."

"Soon, my son."

But I knew I couldn't wait much longer. My son was pale from hunger. I'd bake the best bread possible from our last bit of flour and oil. My baking stone needed to be very hot to bake the bread crisp on the outside and moist on the inside. And I needed to find a good supply of wood to make the stone hot. Quickly, I covered my head and headed outside the city gate.

As I gathered dead branches in my arms, I heard the sound of someone approaching.

"Woman," a voice called. "Could you bring me a little water in a jar. I'm so thirsty."

Standing a few feet from me was a mountain of a man who looked like a walking desert. He was covered with dust and sand. I knew what it was like to be without, so I smiled encouragingly to him. Then I turned to get the water.

"And please," he said. "Bring me a piece of bread."

My heart stopped with my feet. Bread! I swallowed hard. "I don't have any bread." I dropped my head. "I do have a small bit of flour and oil. But it's for my last meal with my son. After that we won't have anything. We'll wait to die."

"Don't be afraid," he said.

I lifted my head. His voice was not like those who told me to worship Baal.

"Go home," he said. "Make a small cake of bread for me from what you have and bring it to me. Then make some for your son and yourself. The God of Israel won't let your jar of flour be used up. He won't let your jug of oil run dry."

Could I trade my last meal for a promise from his God? Yes, this man looked as hungry as I did, but he didn't seem afraid or panicky like me. If he could trust his God for food, I could trust his God too.

The bread turned out perfectly, just as I hoped, speckled brown on both sides and creamy white on the inside. The man, whose name was Elijah, thanked God and then thanked me before putting the sweetness of food on his lips.

As he ate, I went back to check the jar and the jug. There was exactly enough flour and oil to make another bread cake for my son and me! The stone was still hot. This bread cake turned out as good, if not better, than the first one.

My son smiled through his wide eyes. He had peeked in the jug and jar, and they were full *again!* Just as the man from God had promised.

So before we ate, we thanked the God who gave us food through the joy of a miracle.

Something to Think About
Was it easy for the woman to give bread to Elijah?

Something to Read About
You can read about Elijah and the widow in 1 Kings 17:10-16.

Something to Pray About
Lord, thank you for the joy of your gifts. Help us to share with others and to depend on you for what we need. Amen.

trade thirty:

A Helping Hand *for* A Clapping Hand

Steven and Raymond were walking to the park for a soccer game.

"I'm going to play hard and score a goal," said Steven.

"Me too," said Raymond. "Maybe even two goals."

Steven took a drink out of his water bottle. "Or three."

Lyle, the little boy from across the street, called to them. "My ball rolled into the street. Could you get it for me? I'm not allowed to go in the street."

"Can't," Steven said. "We're on our way to a very important soccer game."

"It'll only take a second," Raymond said. He ran over to the ball and rolled it back to Lyle. Then Raymond hurried to catch up with Steven.

They had not gone much farther when they met Timmy blocking the sidewalk with his bicycle.

"Move your bike," Steven said. "We're in a hurry to get to the park."

"But I can't ride it," Timmy said. "The seat is too high. I can't get it to come down."

Steven kicked the bike with his foot and then walked around it.

"I'll help you," Raymond said. "It'll only take a minute."

"I'm not waiting for you," Steven said as he walked away from Raymond, Timmy, and the bike.

Raymond moved the seat all the way down to the crossbar.

Timmy hopped on the bike. "Now it's too low," he said.

Raymond raised the seat up just a bit.

Timmy tried it again. This time it was just right.

Raymond hurried to catch up to Steven, but Steven had already turned the corner at the end of the block.

After Raymond rounded the corner, he almost bumped into Becky Sue who was sitting on the sidewalk, crying.

"Don't step on me like that other boy did," Becky Sue said.

Raymond sat on the sidewalk next to Becky Sue. "Why are you crying?" Raymond asked.

"My shoelaces came untied," cried Becky Sue. "I tripped and fell and skinned my knee."

"You need a Band-Aid," said Raymond. "I'll knock on your door and tell your mother."

Becky Sue's mother cleaned and bandaged the skinned knee. Raymond tied Becky Sue's shoelaces. Then Becky Sue's mother gave Raymond a ride to the park in the car. They arrived at the park just in time for the game.

"How did you get here so fast?" asked Steven.

"My friends gave me a ride," Raymond said.

Steven made the first goal of the game. He jumped around and made lots of noise. "What a beautiful shot," he said, congratulating himself.

A few people clapped for his goal.

A few minutes later, Steven got the ball again. He didn't pass the ball to Raymond who was standing in the right spot to make a goal. Instead Steven kicked the ball toward the goal himself. The ball hit the goal post and bounced back into the field. With a quick and easy tap on the ball, Raymond shot it into the goal.

"Way to go, Raymond!" shouted someone from the sidelines. A big group cheered loudly.

Raymond looked to see who was cheering. Lyle and his family, Timmy and his friends, and Becky Sue and her mother were clapping and jumping for Raymond.

"Some people have all the luck," said Steven.

Raymond waved back at his friends. He felt happy for the rest of the game and scored two more goals.

Something to Think About

Who would you rather have for a friend, Raymond or Steven? Why?

Something to Read About

God loves the person who gives happily. *2 Corinthians 9:7b*

Something to Pray About

Lord, thank you for the opportunities you give us to help others. Don't let us pass them by. Amen.

trade thirty-one:

My Clean River
for
A Dirty One

As the commander of the king's army, I kept the swords sharp and shiny. Last month a sword tip scratched my arm. I didn't feel any pain. That was strange. Then I noticed white spots on my arm. Could it be? I put on a long-sleeved shirt so that my arms were covered.

One day, my servant was going over our daily schedule while I shaved.

"Naaman, sir, you cut yourself."

I touched my face, searching for the cut.

"Didn't you feel it?" he asked.

I rolled up my sleeves and showed him my arms.

"Leprosy," he whispered.

I nodded. "what am I going to do?"

"Sir, what's the king going to do? There's no commander like you."

Soon after the news of my leprosy spread, my wife came to me. "Naaman," she said, "I have good news for you."

"Now that I have leprosy, no news is good."

"Just listen," she said. "My new servant girl, the one you brought back as a prize from the battle against the Israelites, says she knows who can cure leprosy."

These were the first words of hope I had heard. "Who is it?!"

"A prophet from Israel's God. He can cure anything."

"A healer in the land of my enemy! I'll get permission from the king to go to Israel."

My king wrote a note to the king of Israel. Then he sent me on my way, loaded down with gifts for the Israelite king.

Israelites stared at me as I entered their city. Guards followed me to the palace and the king's throne. What did they think a leper without a sword was going to do? They were so afraid of me, they couldn't even feel sorry for me.

With trembling hands, the king took my letter. He read it. Then he tore his clothes. I was seeking hope, and he was throwing a fit. The king screamed. "Am I God? I can't heal you."

A messenger plowed through the mass of upset people. He handed a note to the king.

"Ahem." The king cleared his throat. "It seems we *do* have someone in the kingdom that can cure leprosy. Go to the prophet Elijah."

I climbed back into my chariot. Hope filled my heart once again as my servants hurried the horses and chariots to the home of Elijah.

We turned the last corner. "Whoa," my driver called to the horses.

Before I could step out of my chariot, a servant ran out of the house. Surely he would lead me to his master. The magical ceremony of healing was about to begin!

"Go to the Jordan River," said the servant. "Wash yourself seven times in the river. Then your skin will be like new. The leprosy will be gone."

What! The great man of God didn't even come out to see me? He didn't wave a magic wand or call on the name of his God. Wash in the dirty old Jordan River? Never! If washing in a river would cure me, I'd go to the clear, blue waters of the rivers in my country.

"Sir," said my servant. "If the prophet had asked you to do something great, wouldn't you have done it?"

"I suppose."

"Then why not wash seven times in the river? It couldn't hurt."

My servant was right. We drove down to the river, and I eased myself into the muddy water. I mean muddy and ugly. One, two, three . . . seven times I dipped down. Each time was as nasty as the first. After the seventh time, I wiped the mud off my arms. The deadly, white spots were gone!

I jumped back into my chariot. "Back to Elijah's place," I shouted. "Elijah and his God are awesome."

Elijah wouldn't trade the healing his God gave to me for all the money in the world. With a God as great as his, he didn't need things. But I did ask Elijah for a gift. I asked for as much earth as two of my mules could carry. This dirt would remind me of God's land. I wanted to trade all my gods for worshiping the true God. I'd kneel on this soil and praise God in heaven.

Something to Think About

Why do you suppose God chose to heal Naaman in such a strange way?

Something to Read About

You can read about Naaman in 2 Kings 5:1-19.

Something to Pray About

Dear Lord, help us trust you more than anyone or anything. Help us to obey you in all we do. Amen.

trade thirty-two:

One Too Many *for* The Right Amount

I watched the clock. Any minute now the recess bell would ring.

"Turn in your math papers," said Mrs. Hart, "then you may go out for recess."

I chewed on my pencil. Would my answers be right this time? Probably not. I stuffed the paper into my desk. Pulling my jacket hood over my head, I crept toward the playground door.

"Victoria," called Mrs. Hart. "Did you put your math paper in the finished work box?"

"I'll do it later."

"We need to talk," said Mrs. Hart. "I'm very worried about your math work."

Why was Mrs. Hart worried? Did she have trouble when students didn't give her the right answers?

"Sit in this chair," Mrs. Hart said. She opened a folder. It was full of my math papers. "These red marks tell me you need help in math."

I sat up straight in the chair. I knew getting help was a good idea. Maybe I could get David to help me. He knew how to work his math papers. He worked fast and got the right answers.

"Do you want help?" Mrs. Hart asked.

"Oh, yes," I said.

"Great. I'll send you down to Mrs. Moore in the special classroom. She'll help you every day from ten o'clock to ten-thirty."

I scooted down in my chair. Mrs. Moore would be like any other teacher. She'd ask questions but wouldn't help with the answers.

I could hardly make my feet point in the direction of the special classroom next to the secretary's office. Would the math problems work any better in my head for Mrs. Moore? I didn't think so.

"Come in," said Mrs. Moore. "Mrs. Hart said you were coming today. You're the first one here. Two students are coming from Mrs. Kate's class, three from Mr. Evert's class, and one from Mrs. Hughes' class. Count yourself and set out a pencil for everyone."

I found the pencils in a jar, but how many did I need? There were too many different numbers of students from too many classes. Maybe the right number of pencils was already in the jar. I placed the pencils on the table.

Two noisy boys came in the room followed by four girls.

"Everyone is here," said Mrs. Moore. "Take a seat."

"Who counted the pencils?" asked the brown-haired boy.

"It must have been her," said the tall boy. "She can't count."

I looked at the pencils. There was one pencil too many on the table.

Mrs. Moore sat down in the chair next to the extra pencil. "It looks like Victoria set out a pencil for me. Thank you, Victoria," she said.

"You're welcome," I said. I liked the way she didn't make me feel bad for not doing it right.

Then she showed me how to add the two from Mrs. Kate's class to the three from Mr. Evert's class to the one from Mrs. Hughes' class, and one more for me.

Maybe Mrs. Moore *would* be able to help me. I put all my numbers in a row just as she showed me. I added more twos to threes and fives to sixes. My answers came out the same as Mrs. Moore's answers.

She put a star on the chart beside my name. "I'll see you tomorrow, Victoria," she said. "I think you're going to be a good math student."

Putting numbers together means paying attention to each one. I know that now because Mrs. Moore said so. She wants each number and each person to come out right. She cares about each one of us.

Something to Think About
What was special about Mrs. Moore?

Something to Read About
Give all your worries to God because he cares for you. *1 Peter 5:7*

Something to Pray About
Dear Lord, thank you for giving us teachers like Mrs. Moore to care for us. Help us to always trust you to know what's best for us. Amen.

trade thirty-three:

His Life *for* Yours

When Jesus lived on earth, there were shepherds who lived and worked in the hillsides around the cities. The people Jesus taught knew a lot about the work of a shepherd. They knew how a shepherd climbed steep hills looking for green grass. They knew how a shepherd found shade for his sheep during the hottest part of the day, and how he carried heavy pails of water across the desert to supply their thirsty tongues.

Shepherds also built safe places for their sheep to rest at night. They carried heavy stones and stacked them high enough so that no wild animal could climb over and hurt the sheep. Each night, the shepherd counted his sheep. And when all the sheep were safe inside the walled area, the shepherd protected the entrance from any thieves or robbers by becoming a human door.

When Jesus taught the people about himself, he didn't say, "I'm the great king. You must bring me your money and gold so we can build a spectacular kingdom." No, Jesus said, "I am the good shepherd. I know you by name, like a shepherd knows his sheep."

One day Jesus told a story about a lost sheep.

"Pretend you are a shepherd," Jesus said. "You have one hundred sheep. It's the end of a long day of taking care of the sheep."

If you had been in Jesus' audience that day, you would have started imagining what Jesus was talking about. Maybe you'd think about how brown the grass around the hills of Bethlehem had been during the past few weeks. You could see yourself taking the sheep up to a high spot along the rocky edge. You think about how at night you would be glad to be back home and ready to have the sheep rest safely in the walled pen.

"But one of your sheep is missing," Jesus said. "When you count them as they enter the sheepfold, there are only ninety-nine."

You can feel the panic in your heart. Your cousin lost a sheep last year. You helped him through the long, cold night searching for that lamb.

"The good shepherd will look for the lost sheep," Jesus said.

You nod. That's right. You can't give up because it's late or you're hungry.

"When the shepherd finds the lamb," Jesus said, "he's very happy. He puts it on his shoulders and goes home. He tells his friends that the lost lamb is found. Everyone is happy."

You smile too. You know how it feels to wrap your arms around the bleating, woolly ball. The sheep relaxes in your arms, and you relax too. A lost lamb would soon belong to a wolf if the shepherd didn't find it. You know a shepherd doesn't like to pay a big price for a lamb just to lose it to a wolf.

Then Jesus said something that surprised you. "I'm like the good shepherd. A person who doesn't know God is like the lost lamb."

You feel the panic in your heart again. If you don't know God, then you are lost. You could be in great danger.

"When the lost person comes to know and love God," Jesus said, "then everyone in heaven is happy. They rejoice because the one that was lost is found."

You decide then and there that you will follow Jesus. And you do. You walk in his footsteps wherever he goes.

Then one day, something terrible happens. Jesus is trapped. The people who hate him and hate what he says about God, kill him by hanging him on a cross.

You hide with the other believers. How can you follow this good shepherd now that he is dead?

Then the most wonderful thing happens; he comes back to you. He's alive! Finally, you realize what Jesus did when he died. He paid a price for you.

You couldn't belong to a holy God without paying for the lying, unloving ways of your life. So he traded his life in heaven to come down to earth. Then he traded his life for your punishment. Now you can follow him to heaven.

Something to Think About
How is Jesus like a shepherd to you?

Something to Read About
You can read Jesus' story about the lost sheep in Luke 15:1-10. You can read about Jesus as the good shepherd in John 10:1-21.

Something to Pray About
Dear Jesus, you are the right shepherd to follow. You care about us. You lead us to God in heaven, and we know you have already paid the price to get us into heaven. Thank you. Amen.

trade thirty-four:

Sadness
for
Peace

The sprinkler in the yard next door spun around slowly. I sat on the porch steps watching, waiting for the water to hit the sidewalk on each turn. Drops of water jumped in the air, catching bits of sunlight like jewels.

Inside my house there was no light, no jewels. The shades were pulled down. The light was shut out.

My little sister, Tessa, was dying. No more dancing on the front porch or giggling under the blankets. If only the happiness we shared would return.

A breeze snapped the oak leaves above me. A dog barked; a lawn mower whirred.

Then Dad called me inside. He put his arms around me and told me it was over. Tessa had died.

How could this happen when sisters were for keeping—to share secrets late into the night, my heart cried. *Why couldn't the doctors make the cancer go away?*

For days, there had been no noise in our house. Now it crashed down the doors like an unwelcome visitor.

The phone rang. The doorbell rang. But mostly people just walked in, bringing casserole dishes and red salads with marshmallows.

The minister came next. Voices became still.

He spoke words about Jesus.

One day before she died, when I was sad, Tessa held out her hand to me. I sat on the edge of the bed. We didn't talk for a while; we just held hands.

"Jenny," she said, "am I going to die?"

I couldn't speak. The thought of her dying followed me to school and to bed, but I could never say it.

She held my hand tighter. "It's okay," she said. "I'm going to heaven to be with Jesus. He told me."

The minister's words brought my thoughts back to the room. He was saying something about Jesus. I tried to listen. How did people know when they belonged to Jesus?

I wanted to tug on the minister's sleeve and ask him, but too many people were nodding as if they already knew how it all worked. I should know, too, but I was scared. Tessa would tell me if she was still here.

After a late supper, my mom told me to go to bed. Her eyes were red and swollen, but she gave me a long hug.

I closed the door to my bedroom and sat in the dark. "Please help me, Jesus," I cried. "Please help me know you are real like Tessa said. Help me believe in you. Help me know that Tessa is with you."

My whole body shook. I tried to wrap my arms around myself to stop the shaking.

Then I heard footsteps outside the door of my room. My heart pleaded, *Don't walk away. Hold me. Love me.* And somehow my dad must have heard my silent cry. The door opened, and he tiptoed over to my bed—just as he sometimes did when I should be sleeping, but was just pretending.

He spread his large hand over my back. The gentleness and peace of his touch seeped through his fingertips. He didn't speak. He just sat on the edge of my bed. And he stayed long past the trembling. He stayed until I should have fallen asleep. Then he tiptoed out and gently closed the door.

I didn't want him to leave. I wanted him to stay until the sun brought light back to the earth. I waited for the peace of his hand to leave my body. But it didn't leave. The peace grew stronger; it pressed through my bones and into my heart. It was as if someone else took his place, someone whose peace reached deeper than a parent's ever can.

Who? I whispered.

Jesus, said the voice from my heart.

Something to Think About
Was Tessa afraid to die?

Something to Read About
He who believes in the Son has eternal life. *John 3:36a*

Something to Pray About
Dear Jesus, you have promised that those who love you will live forever. Help us trust you and believe your promises. Amen.